How to coach
SWIMMING

How to coach
SWIMMING

Rick Cross

WILLOW BOOKS
Collins
8 Grafton Street, London W1
1990

Willow Books
William Collins Sons & Co Ltd
London • Glasgow • Sydney • Auckland
Toronto • Johannesburg

First published 1990

A CIP catalogue record for this book is available from the British Library.
ISBN 0 00 218321 8
paperback
ISBN 0 00 218371 4
hardback

Commissioning Editor: Michael Doggart
Senior Editor: Lynne Gregory
Designer: Peter Laws
Illustration: Craig Austin

This book was designed and produced by
Amanuensis Books Ltd
12 Station Road
Didcot
Oxfordshire
OX11 7LL

Originated, printed and bound in Hong Kong by Wing King Tong Co. Ltd

The pronoun 'he' has been used throughout and should be
interpreted as applying equally to men and women as appropriate.
It is important in sport, as elsewhere, that women and men should
have equal status and opportunities.

CONTENTS

INTRODUCTION

Swimming is not just a recreational activity. For many swimmers it is a sport pursued with serious intent, sometimes to Olympic competition standard. This book aims to guide those who wish to coach, whether they be parents encouraging their child to swim or teachers in schools improving the performances of their pupils - perhaps enabling them to participate in a competition. Those who want to obtain nationally-recognized coaching awards should approach the national governing body of the sport, the Amateur Swimming Association (ASA). The ASA is not only responsible for standards and qualifications of coaches, but also a wide range of award schemes designed to encourage people of all ages, abilities and interests (swimming for those with disabilities; diving; synchronized swimming and water polo) to improve their swimming and swim on a regular basis. This book is written, however, with the full cooperation and approval of the ASA and should prove invaluable to swimming coaches of all standards and experience.

Obviously the key to the coach's success is knowledge of fundamental swimming skills. Good coaching, however, requires additional skills. This book is designed to help those who are just learning to coach so that they will be able to assist their pupils in the learning of correct techniques.

It would be marvellous if everyone used their swimming skills in order to learn to save a life, and this is just what the Royal Life Saving Society (RLSS) encourages in its training programmes. As a coach you are urged to take the topic of safety very seriously indeed. If you do you will be able to **enjoy** your swimming coaching in the knowledge that you understand and can fulfil your responsibility to your pupils.

The swimming fraternity differentiates between teachers and coaches. This is not a matter of status but rather one of roles and tasks. Even international swimmers start out as non-swimmers and one cannot come without the other. However, for the sake of clarity and the scope of the series the term 'coach' has been adopted throughout the book. This is not the place for a philosophical debate about the differences. Suffice it to remind ourselves that both are setting out to improve the quality of the performance of their swimmers.

Ideally those who are new to coaching should work with the

supervision and guidance of those more experienced and qualified. Further support is also available from the references given in Chapter 8.

Rick Cross

THE AUTHOR

Rick Cross qualified at Loughborough. He has been an LEA adviser and head of teaching studies in higher education, and is now a freelance lecturer and consultant in education and recreation. He is also a member of several A.S.A. committees and an A.S.A. Principal Tutor.

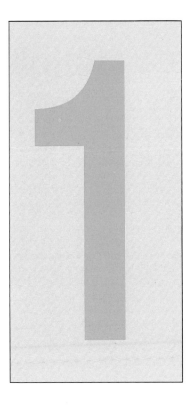

SAFETY IN SWIMMING

Safety in Swimming

The 1974 Health and Safety at Work Act and *Safety in Swimming Pools* both (see book list in Chapter 8) highlight the hazards particular to swimming pools and the responsibilities of those who work in them. Their implementation, however, depends on the vigilance and common sense of those involved in the coaching of swimming. It is impossible to list all the likely areas of concern, but from a coach's point of view they can be classified under:

> **The coach has 5 areas of concern**:
> - Changing accommodation
> - The pool surround
> - In the water
> - Equipment
> - Clarification of responsibilities

• **Changing accommodation** where he should supervise and discipline the swimmers, and ensure that all slippery surfaces, sharp projections or unhygienic conditions are remedied.
• **The pool surround** which includes the points raised above and responsibility for there being depth markings, and clear instructions concerning entry into the water and class assembly points.
• **In the water** where designated swimming areas should be roped off, the conditions for head-first entries made clear and the correct coach-to-pupil ratio in a session observed.
• **Equipment** with swimming aids in good condition and available on the poolside.
• **Clarification of responsibilities** when they are likely to be divided, for example with a visiting school class and teacher, should be clearly understood by all concerned. It might be that the swimming coach appointed by the Local Education Authority (LEA) is in charge of safety in and near the water as well as the teaching, while the school teacher is responsible for the other areas of concern. Clarification of the prescise responsibilities is essential for the safety of the pupils.

The Coach and Safety

In the introduction, reference was made to lifeguarding and the Royal Life Saving Society (RLSS). Whilst the terms 'lifeguarding' and 'life saving' are related, they are not to be confused. In spite of all the hard work done by the RLSS, many people still think of the dramatic rescue as the true stuff of lifeguarding!

As a swimming coach, however, you will only be of real value to your pupils if you remember that good lifeguarding involves not only close supervision of your swimmers and a personal awareness of the possible dangers in swimming, but a responsibility to educate your charges on matters of safety. There comes a time when young children, with much trepidation on their parents' part, have to cross a major road on their own. But they do so after a rigorous education programme from parents, teachers, the police and other safety organizations. And so it is with swimming. There will come a time when children will go swimming without the watchful eye of parents and teachers. If the youngsters are aware of the dangers, they not only reduce risks for themselves, they also reduce the risk to others who might have to help them out of difficult circumstances.

Lifeguarding works to lessen the chances of a serious incident occurring - it does not totally remove the possibility. There should never be any complacency about the matter of safety, not even with the strongest of swimmers in your care. Remember, there is a difference between swimming in a warm indoor pool and in open water. The difference is not only the danger from tides and currents but also the cold, particularly in the open waters of the UK. Warning your swimmers of that danger alone might well stop a tragedy occurring, particularly at holiday time.

To be a safe coach you should:

Be alert at all times
Always keep your eyes on the group in the water. Incidents happen in fractions of a second, and turning one's back on the pupils in order to talk to a parent or to get a float or other equipment, is a dangerous practice.

Be aware of:
• Water depths and the area available in each depth - and make certain that the class know these areas. Use ropes to divide the pool not only for organizational purposes, but also to give weak swimmers the chance to hang onto a support should they need one;
• The number of swimmers in your group. Count them in and

count them out!
• Water and air temperatures;
• The abilities of your group;
• Any medical problems that might affect individuals whilst they are in the water;
• The need to allow a reasonable time between eating and entering the water. Swimming too soon after eating causes a swimmer distress and may result in him being sick;
• The dangers of chewing and eating whilst swimming;
• The dangers of fooling, running on the poolside, shouting and throwing people into the water;
• Your own abilities and fitness;
• Your own lifeguarding/life saving skills and those of others with whom you work, and who might be of assistance in an emergency;
• Any pool rules and LEA regulations concerning the conduct of swimming groups, particularly those concerning responsibilities in staff/pupil ratios and the swimming ability of those in charge of groups;
• Emergency procedures which should be known before an incident occurs:
    - find out if there is an emergency button or buzzer and what support it will bring;
    - locate the telephone and note the positioning of the safety equipment. Remember entering the water in a rescue is the last resort;
    - if there are whistle drills find out what they mean.

An emergency, by definition, means that you will have to act fast and will have no time to investigate procedures. The only thing you will find out is whether you can cope - a sobering thought!
If you do get involved in an incident, no matter how insignificant it may seem, always make and keep notes about it. They could be useful in the subsequent treatment of the victim, or in any legal implications which might arise.

Entering the water is a last resort. Use other methods whenever possible.
Tow with thumb and forefinger. Flex other three fingers up towards the centre of chin and keep clear of the throat.

Summary

To be a safe coach you should:
1. Be alert and aware at all times.
2. Be able to
   • observe carefully
   • recognize the need for help
   • recover somebody in need of help
   • resuscitate when the occasion demands.
   Get the observation right and your other abilities may not be tested.

For further reading material and information on safety in swimming see Chapter 8.

THE WORK OF THE COACH

The Work of the Coach

Qualifications to Coach

The coaching qualifications of the national governing body (ASA) are much sought after because as the certificates of the national governing body of the sport they are accepted by most local authorities, especially the education authorities, as a national standard of competence.

Courses for the certificates are tutored by people who have been trained and qualified after a series of rigorous courses, and assessment or examination is carefully carried out by qualified people. In this way there is a national system of quality control via senior and principal tutors.

The certificate system is structured in a hierarchical way and covers all aspects of the sport. There are awards to cover coaching in swimming (including working with people with disabilities), synchronized swimming, water polo and diving and these certificates are constantly under review to take into account new knowledge and techniques.

Learning to Coach

Coaches have perfectly normal human failings which in most cases need to be overcome if they are going to be effective in their role. Coaches develop their skills in the following areas:

Knowledge of
• Swimming in general;
• Stroke analysis;
• Stroke mechanics;
• How learners learn;
• How to coach.

Communication
With their pupils by means of
• The voice;
• The use of visual images/demonstrations (watching another

swimmer; using a video or a chart etc);
• Manually helping a swimmer through the correct pattern of movement (usually used sparingly and probably as a last resort). Most coaches probably use a combination of voice and some sort of demonstration as their normal means of communicating ideas and points to their swimmers;
• Encouraging feedback from the pupils;
With other teachers/coaches.

Relationships
• Understand their swimmers' needs;
• Encourage their swimmers with positive teaching points;
• Gain their swimmers' confidence;
• Be reliable and have a professional approach;
• Get on with other coaches.

Organisation
• Have an overall scheme;
• Relate individual sessions to the overall scheme;
• Plan individual sessions to take account of:
  - the time available
  - the water space available
  - the number, age, background and ability of the members of the group
  - the equipment available
  - the water/air temperatures
  - progress made during previous sessions, which should be recorded for this reason.

Assessment
• Through careful observation of their swimmers;
• By analysing their pupils' swimming skills;
• Through evaluation of their own coaching performance and the progress made in both individual sessions and the overall coaching scheme;
• By discussion, both formal and informal, with other coaches in order to consider and test ideas for future use.

Understanding the Learning Process

There are a great many stories circulating about learning to swim by being thrown in the deep end and having to cope. The success rate of this method of learning to swim can, at best, be described as dubious.

The most successful process for learning most things, and swimming is no exception, is the so-called 'whole-part-whole' method. This means that the coach allows the swimmer to experience as near to the total activity as can be reasonably expected, after which it is broken down into more manageable parts upon which to focus, before these parts are put back into the whole context again.

This method will obviously have certain limitations in some instances. It would be unfortunate if a young child suddenly announced that he wished to take up diving and was directed to the ten-metre board to attempt the 'whole', with a view to later working on the manageable parts.This clearly would not come within the bounds of the reasonably expected.

The learning process is most successful when there is:

• **Enjoyment** so the pupils come back for more.
• **Understanding** such that the pupils know what they are trying to achieve.
• **Positive feedback** with pupils being told what they should aim to do next time rather than what not to do.
• **Clarity of explanation** with just one point of instruction given at a time.
• **Encouragement** to show that good efforts have been noticed, rather than weaknesses emphasized and berated.
• **Repetition of drills and exercises** is encouraged and time allowed for it. In order to improve, only correct practice makes perfect so there should be plenty of positive feedback from the coach. It is probable that each session will be a slightly-modified version of a previous session in order to reinforce the learning that took place.
• **Safety** such that pupils are secure in the knowledge that they are unlikely to come to any harm. Fear inhibits the learning process.
• **Confidence** in the coach and in his ability to teach.
• **A pleasant atmosphere** in which the pupils feel comfortable.
• **Activity** with lots of practical exercises, which should be interspersed with, but not dominated by, listening and seeing.
• **Variety** allowing the pupils to try out a range of ideas and activities to help overcome learning difficulties and maintain their interest.
• **Demonstration of new activities** to help the pupils better understand what they are trying to do.

Planning the Coaching Session

While there is clearly no one correct way to coach, it is important that the coach is aware of the fundamental aim of teaching which is to work to improve the quality of the pupils' performance whatever their level of competence. Progress will be made faster by some pupils than others, and the coach should set out a programme for improvement which takes into account these individual differences.

Each session should be regarded as one of a series and should therefore be related to previous and succeeding sessions. It should have:

• An aim which is related to an overall scheme;
• An introductory activity which should be an uncomplicated and brief start to the session;
• A development of an activity which will probably be an opportunity to reinforce previously-learned skills or to introduce new skills, and should be based on a central theme or task;
• A concluding activity in which the pupils could practise something of their own, or an activity which contrasts with what has gone before. All must be supervised;
• Notes on the equipment which will be required like floats, armbands etc;
• Evaluation notes which act as a record of the achievements of individuals as well as a self-evaluation by the coach;
• Be organised with regard to the appropriate safety points raised in Chapter 1.

For those who have little or no experience in session planning, a suggested layout for what is known as an orthodox session, might look like the example opposite. It is probably best done on an A4 sheet used horizontally, with session evaluation notes on the reverse side.

Notes

1. Note any special problems or considerations which might play a part in the session's structure.

2. Note whether the group is being introduced to a new skill, like a new stroke, or if it is a development or improvement on the work of a previous session.

3. Keep explanations of exercises simple and brief, for example ' a width of full stroke' or 'a width legs only with float'.

4. It is difficult to lay down hard and fast rules about the proportional allocation of time for this because so much depends on the level of the swimmers concerned. If, for example, the session was about 20 to 25 minutes in length and for improvers, then perhaps the introductory activity would be about three minutes long, the main theme practiced for 15 minutes with the remainder of the session devoted to the concluding activity. If the session was for a very strong group of swimmers then introductory work would probably become more of a physiological 'warm up', and would therefore need to be longer. The main part of the session would take up more time and the concluding activity might be in the form of a 'swim down'. It is important to remember that it is not necessarily the length of a session that determines whether or not the targets are achieved, it is the quality and quantity of work done.

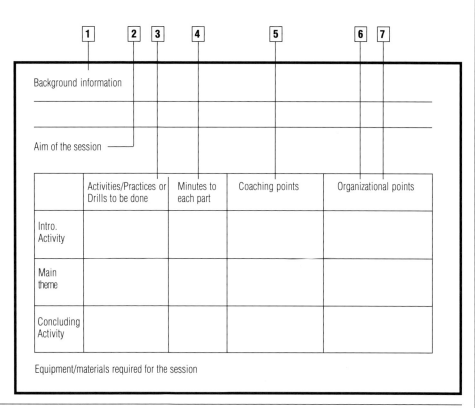

	Activities/Practices or Drills to be done	Minutes to each part	Coaching points	Organizational points
Intro. Activity				
Main theme				
Concluding Activity				

Background information

Aim of the session

Equipment/materials required for the session

5. These are the points you will probably need to emphasize: for example, that the body should be flat in the water or that the hand should enter the water near or on the centre line of the body.

6. Will the group enter the water all at once, two at a time or one by one? When and how the floats will be distributed can also be noted in this column. Will the group always work as one unit or will it be subdivided into ability sections?

7. The place of demonstration, the timing of it and its presentation to the group needs thought. For effective learning to occur the demonstrations should happen as close to the group's own attempts at the skill as possible, so that they observe, then try. Sometimes, water and air temperatures might mean that the observing has to be done at the beginning of the session before the group enters the water, so that there is a time lag between observation and

the pupils' attempts. Clearly there has to be a trade-off in such cases. The presentation of the demonstration should take into account:
• Why it is being done
• What the observers are supposed to see
• What the observers are supposed to hear
• Where the coach and the group stand for it to be most effective
• Where the group stand in relation to what is being demonstrated.

21

THE WORK OF THE COACH

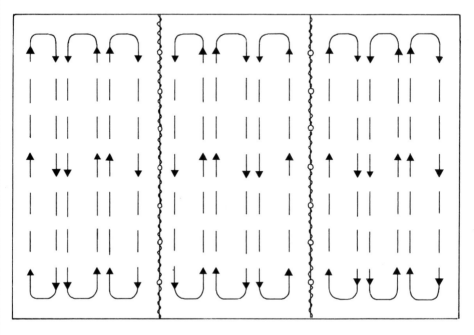

Lane or chain swimming needs to be well disciplined for safety.

Other ways in which swimming sessions can be organized are outlined below:

1. Stroke schedule session Schedules covering the range of ability levels in the group are set to help the swimmers reinforce techniques learned in the previous session. The coach provides feedback on an individual basis whilst the swimmers work through the schedule.

2. Time/distance session Swimmers are set specific distances to cover, or a specific period of time to swim, and the results are recorded as a means of assessing progress.

3. Lane schedules The workloads are likely to be greater and will probably cover a variety of strokes, performed under a range of stresses, to improve not only technique but also endurance and strength. For the more able swimmer.

4. Recreational session The emphasis is less on formal stroke-work and more on other fun activities involving some lesser-known strokes (perhaps even making some up) or games and races. For occasional use.

Whichever of these methods you use, remember that the value of the work involved depends on the quality of the swimmers' techniques in the first place. It follows, therefore, that these sessions should follow a number of orthodox technique-improvement sessions. It should also be noted that, for these sessions to work well, the coach will have to work extremely hard. If a swimmer with poor technique is allowed to swim for any length of time without feedback, their incorrect actions will simply be reinforced and become even more difficult to correct as a consequence.

For those coaches who are new to swimming it is probably easier to start by using the orthodox type of session. But remember, never swim the fun out of swimming.

Summary

Coaches need to develop their:
• Knowledge of the swimming strokes and coaching as well as understanding how pupils learn best;
• Communication skills;
• Relationships with their pupils and other coaches;
• Organisational skills;
• Assessment abilities of the swimmer's progress and problems.

Planning the session
Every session should have:
• An aim
• An introductory 'warm-up' session
• A main activity which reinforces previously learned skills
• A concluding activity

All of these should be supervised. This forms the basis of an orthodox swimming session. There are other ways in which it can be organized, but these are only of use to more able swimmers and should come after a series of orthodox swimming sessions. They include:
• A stroke schedule session
• A time/distance session
• Lane schedules
• A recreational schedule.

TEACHING THE NON-SWIMMER

Teaching the Non-swimmer

Before discussing coaching in detail, it might be useful to consider a definition of a swimmer:

A swimmer is one who has the ability to travel, say five metres,* preferably horizontally and on the surface of the water, without recourse to swimming aids of any description, and without resting, stopping, touching the side or bottom of the pool, by any combination of limb movements.

While anyone who can complete the above test is a swimmer, it is clearly too general a description from which to prepare coaching material for a session. What usually happens is that swimmers are classified as beginners, learners, improvers, middle improvers, advanced improvers and so on - the descriptive vocabulary may vary slightly from one locality to another.

* a purely arbitrary distance

Coach and Pupil Relationships

Non-swimmers come in all shapes, sizes and ages. It is probably in the coaching of the non-swimmer that that you will experience some of your greatest frustrations; very often there will appear to be nothing to prevent the pupil from swimming, apart from fear. However, few coaches could deny that the satisfaction gained from helping a non-swimmer to become a swimmer is enormous.

The previous comment regarding the importance of a congenial learning environment applies particularly to the non-swimmer. He is likely to be feeling very apprehensive and insecure so it is essential that the coach works hard to reassure him and put him at his ease. A comfortable air and water temperature, colourful aids and supports and a safe swimming area help enormously, but nothing helps as much as an encouraging, cheerful coach.

The Adult Non-swimmer

The courage required by an adult to present himself publicly as a non-swimmer, and the possible embarrassment he may feel, is considerable. Any coach who finds himself working with adults should respect this courage. It is helpful to try and find out why the adult did not learn when he was younger. It might be a fear of water or an accident, or something as simple as a lack of facilities where he was brought up. Whatever the reason, he has come to swimming later rather than earlier and is likely to be highly motivated.

He will probably prefer to work in a small group, away from a crowd. It is possible that his joints and muscles will not respond as those of a younger person and the coach will have to make allowances for this. Furthermore, the adult will need more detailed explanations about the nature of what he is being asked to do, and it might be that he will benefit greatly from individual attention. He will certainly appreciate understanding and a sense of humour on the part of the coach.

The Use of Swimming Aids

Swimming aids come in a variety of forms. Inflatable arm bands and rings (the latter are perhaps less common these days) and polystyrene floats of different sizes, shapes and colours are probably the most popular forms of support used. The list is extended by adding buoyant, but not inflatable, waist supports, bar-bell shaped floats and a host of highly coloured toy-like objects which encourage play both on the surface and under it.

Coaches differ in their opinions about the value of swimming aids in the coaching of non-swimmers. Here are the essential arguments for and against their use:

The arguments AGAINST their use

1. The use of swimming aids and supports makes the non-swimmer reliant upon them and as a consequence there may be problems in weaning them off.

2. Swimming aids can hinder the correct limb movements or body position and slow down the learning process.

3. The inflatable type of aids take time to blow up and need good maintenance and storage to ensure that they remain in good condition.

The arguments FOR their use

1. Bearing in mind that swimming is the process of travelling horizontally through the water, anything which enables the non-swimmer to experience this early on is likely to speed up his learning.

2. Swimming aids help non-swimmers to appreciate that water is supportive and that some of the early arm and leg movements actually cause them to travel. Early success is important to the learning of any new activity.

3. The argument about the 'weaning' problem is offset by the expected role of the coach. Just as he 'sells' the swimming aid as the way to success in the early stages so, later, he should persuade his pupils that they are getting in the way and so encourage their removal.

4. The argument concerning the time taken to inflate the aids raises the question of whether they actually need to be deflated at all. If there is sufficient storage space then time can be saved by simply leaving them inflated.

In practice, good coaches adapt themselves to the needs of the individual non-swimmer and make decisions about the use of swimming aids on these grounds, rather than taking an inflexible and dogmatic stance one way or the other. Generally speaking, the evidence supports the use of swimming aids.

Swimming aids come in a variety of forms, as shown in the illustrations opposite.

The Aim of the Coach

While the objective is obviously to teach the non-swimmer to swim, the emphasis should always be on activity and fun. Precise limb movements and breathing practices are far less important in these early stages. Swimming aids will probably prove very useful but remember their use should be dictated by the individual concerned. Early exercises for the non-swimmer should get him to move in the water as soon as possible, using any means that give enjoyment. Many years ago the ASA introduced the slogan, 'Swimming is good fun!'

To this one might add, 'If they are laughing, they are probably learning to come to terms with water.'

The Process of Teaching

For reasons of safety, such as the clarity of the overall view of the class, speed of reaction and general class control and discipline, the coach should always work from the poolside, never in the water. If a coach does decide to work in the water for any special reason - for example, if a learner has a particular and serious difficulty - then provision must be made for another coach to be in charge of the group from the poolside. Obviously, if the coach is working with only one non swimmer, one to one, then there are probably many occasions when being in the water would be beneficial.

Step 1 : Getting the Non-swimmer into the Water

There are a number of considerations when getting your non-swimmer to step into the water. The process should be:
• As unfussy as possible;
• As much fun as possible;
• Well organized, with as little standing around as possible;

Usually early entries are made backwards via the steps, as illustrated opposite.

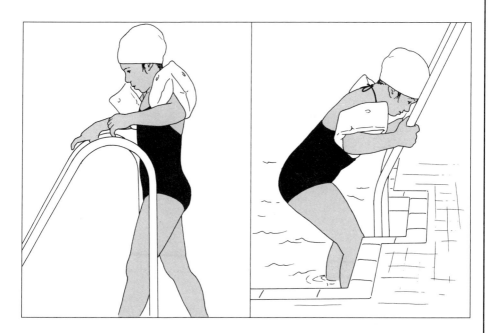

• Perceived by the pupils as being safe and secure (see Chapter 1 for safety notes).

The entry into the water should be organized so that everything that is likely to be needed by the coach is close at hand. If you have a number of pupils and swimming aids are to be used, a carefully thought out system of issuing and fitting them is also needed. Issue systems that require every member of the group to go to the same spot can cause hold-ups and chaos, particularly if that one spot is in a small store-room or cupboard.

Usually, early entries are made via steps with the pupil wearing an inflatable swimming aid and additional floats available within easy reach. At this stage it is vital that the coach exudes confidence and has a pleasant, smiling, reassuring manner. The steps should be climbed down backwards with the pupil's back facing the water. When the pupil has built up more confidence then entry

Later, entries from sitting on the pool-side can be attempted.

can be made from the poolside rather than the steps. To do this the pupil should sit on the poolside facing the water, pass his arms across the body to the right or left and, taking his weight on his hands and turning his back to the water, gently lower himself in.

Once in the water the pupil should be encouraged to move himself around in activities such as walking along holding the rail, or following the edge of the pool round and back again, or even walking across the pool to the other side (assuming, of course, that the appropriate division ropes are in place). This walking exercise could be repeated several times at the same pace, and then gradually speeded up so that the final exercise might require them to run across.

Young children particularly enjoy playing 'motorbikes', that is walking or running in any direction in the roped-off area holding the float on the water surface and using it as a 'handlebar'. They may even accompany this little bit of fantasy with the appropriate sound effects! Some non-swimmers might even have a go at using a leg kicking action whilst others prefer to keep in contact with the side or bottom of the pool.

When coaching a class, be careful not to measure the progress of an individual against that of another, but relative to his last performance. Often progress is almost imperceptible. Tension on the face of a pupil in one session which is replaced by a smile at the next session, even though the exercise practised is the same, is progress for that individual. Another pupil in the same group might have managed a gliding movement with a float over a distance of two metres for the first time. Goading with phrases like, 'You're the only one who can't do it!', are not helpful and simply underline the individual's own personal sense of fear, frustration or even failure. Think positive: 'build 'em up, don't knock 'em down!'

Further class practices with the pupil still using the swimming aid could take the form of races. In competitions to see who can be first across the pool it doesn't matter whether the pupil walks, runs, kicks or flaps his ears - it's simply a game to get across. Several of the less adventurous might take part but still retain a one-handed hold on the rail. The important point is that he is working alongside the group at his own level. Having set a competition, no matter how insignificant the result might seem, a result must be declared.

Depending on the size of the group, it may be necessary to number the pupils alternately 'one' or 'two' and send them off in waves at different times. This not only reduces overcrowding in the space available but offers more variety of competition, provides the coach with the time to note individual progress and the non-swimmers with intervals in which to gain breath. To add variety you could place the 'ones' and 'twos' on the opposite sides of the pool and set them in competition to see who can reach the other side first. Again, the method of travel is largely irrelevant, except that they are not to get out of the water! This sort of activity can increase the decision-making problems for the coach because of the need to declare a winner, but it can create a lot of enjoyment.

Coincidentally, an offshoot of the above activities is that the pupil experiences getting his face wet. This is further encouraged by setting tasks that involve pushing small plastic balls around the pool, first with the chin, then with the nose, later with the forehead and finally with the hair. These games are more productive than employing the age-old cry of the swimming teacher, 'Get your face wet! Go on, there's nothing to it!' This phrase must be the one most dreaded by the non-swimmer anticipating their first visit to the pool.

Swimming with the face in the water is essential in order to swim well, but it is not a prerequisite of learning to swim and should not be made the focus of the non swimmer's attention. There are many far more interesting, exciting and fun things to practise which have the same end result. Interestingly, the 'Let's wash our faces!' game sometimes played with non-swimmers often has the same effect at home with the face remaining unwashed if a similar demand is made by a parent!

Step 2 : Introducing the Swimming Actions

As the non-swimmer learns to come to terms with water and begins to enjoy himself through a variety of activities, so the need to work on an efficient method of moving through the water will grow. Exercises which use different kinds of limb movements will help the non-swimmer to see that it is possible to obtain propulsion through the water. At this stage they will probably still be using some kind of swimming aid. If it is of the inflatable variety then, perhaps as confidence grows, it would be appropriate to reduce the amount of air inside.

Follow up these exercises with a programme of stretching, at first over very short distances towards the teacher on the poolside (see cautionary note page 30), then later gliding over longer distances using a vigorous pushing action. Learning to push and glide, first with the swimming aids and later without, are vital steps to becoming more horizontal in the water. Gradually the previously-attempted limb movements should be added in to increase propulsion.

Up to this point, the emphasis has been on activity and fun. The fun element must not be lost, but the limb movements and body positions used hitherto might have been inefficient. Just like the racing cyclist who is streamlined to reduce the effect of air hitting his body, so the swimmer moves most effectively when he is horizontal and offering the least resistance to the water. Encourage the swimmer to get as close to the horizontal position in the water as possible either on his front (prone position) or on his back (supine position). Whilst most non-swimmers will probably start on their fronts, some may make better progress and be more comfortable on their backs. It is also likely that the leg movements which they will find easiest to perform will be the up-and-down, alternating kick of the kind used in front crawl swimming, together with an alternating arm-pulling action under the water. This kind of stroke is now known as the 'front paddle', and was formerly known as the 'dog paddle'.

Swimming as near to the horizontal as possible reduces resistance.

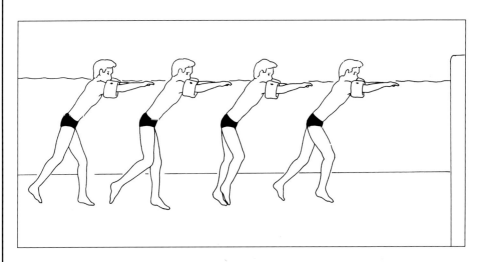

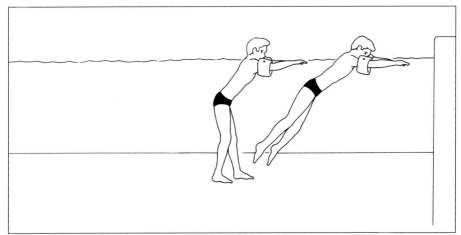

Top left: Walking and stretching for the wall towards the teacher.
Left and above: Increase the distances and remove the support as confidence grows.

Step 3 : The First Swimming Strokes

The Front Paddle

Body position: As near to the horizontal as possible. In the early learning stages the swimmer will probably swim with his head up. Later, as confidence increases, the face will be lowered closer to the water making his position in the water more horizontal.

Leg action: Legs stretched out and as close to the horizontal as possible. The kick should start at the hip, and travel down through the knee, the stretched ankle and through to the stretched toes. The kick should be as deep as the thickness of the body. The legs should be kept straight and long, although some bending at the knee is inevitable. As one leg is driving down, the other is on its way back up in readiness for the next downward movement. The upward movement should end as the heel breaks the surface. This type of leg action is called an alternating kick.

Arm action: Starting from a full stretch ahead of the shoulder, one hand is pressed down and back towards and under the body. The wrist is held firm, with the elbow bent, and the hand acting as a paddle pulling/pushing back towards the feet. The result of this backward movement of the hand is that the swimmer travels forwards.

Whilst one hand is acting in the propulsive phase, the other is recovering under the surface in readiness for its next propulsive phase. In the recovery phase the hand is brought forward close to the chest, with the fingers stretched, on its way back to the full-stretch starting-position directly in front of the shoulder.

Breathing: At this stage breathing techniques are not that important. Natural survival instincts ensure that air comes from somewhere! However, if it is decided to emphasize any particular aspect of breathing make it the need for vigorous exhalation.

Timing/Coordination: Not critical but mention the need to maintain the movements described above.

There is a similar type of stroke done on the back, called the 'back paddle'.

Front paddle
Powerful pressing downwards and backwards movements of the hands are followed by a reaching and stretching forward action.

The Back Paddle

Body position: As near to the horizontal as possible. The body should be straight with the back of the head 'resting' on the water and the eyes looking directly upwards or slightly towards the feet. To keep this position, emphasize the need to keep the hips up.

Leg action: The kick is initiated at the hips and should travel through the knees and ankles to the toes with the final movement upwards completed when the toes break the water surface. Encourage the swimmer to keep his legs straight and long, but, as in the front paddle, there will inevitably be some knee bend. This movement is also an alternating kick.

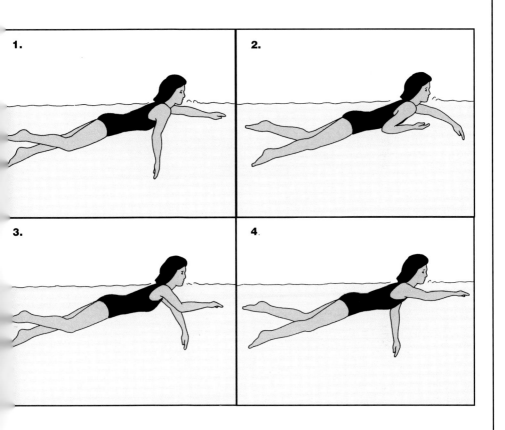

1.

2.

3.

4.

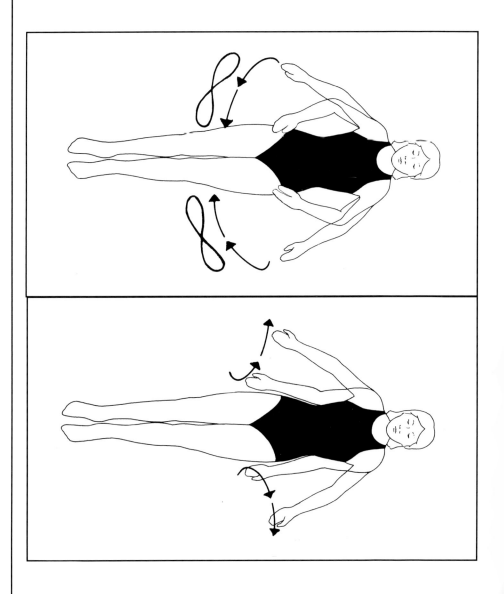

The figure of eight movement of the hands.

Arm action: Initially a large arm movement with both arms working simultaneously making sweeping, pushing movements towards the feet. Whilst this is a reasonable movement for a new swimmer to attempt, it has the disadvantage of an awkward recovery phase which creates excessive resistance. As the swimmer gains confidence, the elbows should be kept closer to the body so that much of the movement is at the wrist. The most efficient way to use the hands is to make movements in a 'figure of eight' above or close to the thighs. Start with the palms facing down and press them down in the water, rotating or tilting the wrists so that the palms pass through facing each other to a point where they are almost facing upwards before returning to the initial position with the palms facing downwards. This 'figure of eight' action is more properly known as 'sculling', and has many uses in swimming.

Breathing: Even less of a problem than in the front paddle above, but if emphasis is to be made, make it the need for vigorous exhalation.

Timing/Coordination: Again not critical but mention the need to maintain the movements described above.

While coaching the front and back paddle movements, encourage the pupil to use a swimming aid and make sure that the learning process is always fun. Have push and glide competitions, ask to see who can make the biggest or smallest splash with a leg kick, set up a series of hoops to rest vertically at the bottom of the shallow part of the pool for the pupils to swim through, have competitions to guess the number of fingers held up by the partner underwater - anything that is fun and makes the pupil more confident in the water. This might well lead to what is later described as the 'multi-stroke' method.

The movement is started by raising the head and pressing down with the hands.

Learning to Stand in the Water

Once the non-swimmer is joining in activities which require the feet to be off the bottom of the pool, it is important that, at the same time, he learns how to regain the standing position. In the early stages of learning, trying to stand up could well be a panic measure. If it is not done firmly and safely, the learner can become insecure about exercises in which he has to take his feet off the bottom of the pool and this can severely hold up his progress.

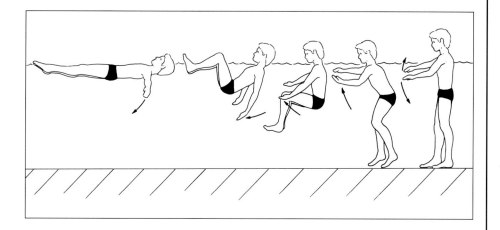

Regaining the feet from the front (prone) position involves:
1. Raising the head.
2. Pressing firmly downwards with the hands.
3. Bending the knees and bringing them forwards under the body in a tucked or curled position.
4. Stretching the feet down towards the bottom of the pool and, when they are below the body, planting them down squarely and firmly.

Most of the work is done with a scooping action of the hands.

Regaining the feet from the back (supine) position involves:
1. Bringing the chin forwards onto the chest.
2. Moving the hands outwards and backwards in a circular motion followed by a downwards and forwards scooping action towards the hips.
3. Bending the knees and lowering the hips to come into a tucked or curled position.
4. Stretching the feet downwards towards the bottom of the pool and, when they are below the body, planting them down squarely and firmly.

Summary

As a coach of the non-swimmer you must:

- Try to understand the difficulties and fears of this level of swimmer;
- Approach the task with a variety of activities;
- Emphasize the FUN element;
- Provide the security of environment they need (see the safety section in Chapter 1);
- Measure progress against the individual concerned, not the class in general.

The steps in the learning process are:

1. To get the nonswimmer in the water, first by the steps then by lowering himself in from the side, and to get him moving around and enjoying the water.

2. Introduce the swimming actions, probably with the use of swimming aids with which he should learn to push and glide on the surface of the water.

3. The first swimming strokes of the front and/or back paddle should be mastered.

4. At the same time he should learn to stand up safely in the water from the horizontal position.

COACHING THE SWIMMER

Coaching the Swimmer

In the previous chapter on coaching the non-swimmer it was suggested that the pupil should be encouraged to experiment with a variety of swimming movements. This is the basis of the 'multi-stroke' method of coaching. By this method the swimmer is given the opportunity to try out different strokes and combinations of limb movements to find the one which will give them the most initial success. Sometimes the other method of working, the 'single stroke', can lead to frustration if the stroke chosen by the coach causes difficulties for the learner. This applies particularly when the coach has indicated that another stroke will not be attempted until the current one has been mastered.

The sense of achievement gained by swimmers learning by the multi-stroke method is very useful to their future learning, although from an organizational point of view the method does present extra problems for the coach. If pool space and design permit, it is often helpful to group the class according to the strokes each of the individuals show a desire to learn, rather than mix the strokes in the working area. If they are grouped like this then coaching points and practices can be used more effectively according to the strokes being taught.

The Application of General Principles

Before looking at the individual strokes in detail it is helpful to introduce two topics which have general application in the coaching of swimming.

1. Stroke mechanics
Efficient swimming is based on good body position:
• As near to the horizontal as possible
• As flat as possible with the head in natural alignment with the spine

Note
Remember, when swimming the hands give the appearance of moving over a considerable distance, whereas, in fact, the body is actually moving past the hands. It is, therefore, essential that limb movements are performed accurately in order to obtain the most efficient equal and opposite reaction from the body.

• As streamlined as possible
The above allow for:
• The minimum of resistance
• The maximum of forward travel
• The minimum of effort and energy expenditure
Factors which detract from efficiency:
• The demands of the stroke being swum
• The individual swimmer's
  - build
  - buoyancy
  - joint mobility
  - confidence
  - strength.

The Application of Stroke Mechanics

Consider Newton's third law of motion : 'For every action there is an equal and opposite reaction'. When applied to swimming it means, for example, that if the hand is pressed backwards in the direction of the feet, the swimmer will travel forwards.

2. Stroke analysis

This, as seen in the descriptions of the first two paddle strokes, is generally approached under these headings:
• Body position
• Leg action : propulsion
                recovery
• Arm action : propulsion
                recovery
• Breathing
• Timing :   coordination
              relationship of legs, arms and breathing

This analysis is often referred to in the coaching of swimming by the mnemonic BLABT.

3. Fault Finding

Coaches should try and adopt a fault-finding approach to the task of providing their swimmers with feedback about their performance:

• Decide on the major fault needing attention
• Decide on the major cause of that fault
• Decide on the appropriate feedback to enable the swimmer to reduce or eradicate that fault.

The examples on the facing page are not exhaustive and should be read in conjunction with the contents of Chapter 5.

Deciding on the First Stroke

When deciding how to introduce the various strokes to the learner, it is useful to know the advantages and disadvantages of each of them. Breaststroke has the advantage of allowing the swimmer to make considerable progress without having to worry about breathing with the face in the water. However, it also happens to be a very complex stroke in its limb movements and in the coordination that is required.

Front crawl, on the other hand, to be swum well, requires the face to be in the water, but the limb movements are less complex. In fact, sometimes it is likened to a walking action. Backstroke movements are also simple, and the face is clear of the water, but many people in the early stages do not like having their ears in the water. Some people also feel very insecure about having to go backwards.

The butterfly is a reasonably complex stroke which requires the face to be in the water to be done properly. In addition, the stroke makes more physical demands on the swimmer and these probably make it a little too difficult for the learner.

It is likely, therefore, that the first stroke to be attempted with most effect will be the front crawl. The word 'likely' is used deliberately because the philosophy behind the multi-stroke approach to coaching is that the swimmer pursues the stroke which he uses most successfully.

Right: A general approach to fault finding.

Possible Fault	**Possible Cause**

1. The swimmer is not horizontal and streamlined	• The nature of the stroke being swum
	• The swimmer's knowledge of the stroke
	• Head position
	  - too high (fear?)
	  - too low
	  - excessive movement (breathing problems?)
	• Leg kick
	  - inaccurate
	  - weak
	• Coordination of limb movements poor

2. The swimmer's leg kick is not contributing to the stability of the body position	• Inaccurate movemements • Weak movements • Coordination of limb movements poor
3. The leg kick is not contributing to the swimmer's propulsion	• The nature of the stroke being swum (usually breaststroke legs contribute more than the arm action) • Inaccurate movements • Weak movements • Coordination of limb movements poor
4. The swimmer's arm action is not the major propulsive force	• The nature of the stroke being swum (usually breaststroke swimmers gain most propulsion from the legs) • Swimmer's knowledge of the stroke • Inaccurate movements • Weak movements • Coordination of limb movements poor
5. The swimmer's breathing is not providing an effective exchange of air	• Fear/tension • Lack of knowledge of head position • Coordination of the breathing and arm action poor
6. The timing of the various parts of the stroke is not accurate and the swimmer is unable to make smooth and effective progress through the water	• Lack of knowledge of the correct coordination • Inability to coordinate movements • Difficulty in performing one or more aspects of the stroke • Fear and tension through being encouraged to attempt too much, too soon • Fatigue (breathing?) • Swimmer too cold

Summary

The multi-stroke method of learning allows the swimmer to pursue whichever stroke he feels most comfortable with to develop his swimming skills.

Swimming is based on good stroke mechanics: that is, a streamlined body position in the water which provides:
• Minimum resistance to the water
• Maximum forward travel
• Minimum effort and energy expenditure.

Swimming strokes are described under the headings:
• Body position
• Leg action, propulsion and recovery
• Arm action, propulsion and recovery
• Breathing
• Timing, coordination of arms, legs and breathing.

Fault finding

The approach to fault finding and providing swimmers with feedback about their performance is:
• Decide on the major fault
• Decide on the major cause of the fault
• Decide on the appropriate feedback to enable the swimmer to reduce or eradicate the fault.

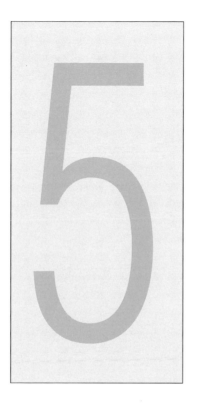

COACHING THE STROKES

Coaching the Strokes

1. Front Crawl

This is the fastest and most efficient stroke. The body can be used in its most streamlined position and at the same time allow for the limbs to be used in the most efficient way. It is generally known as an alternating stroke.

Body position:
• Streamlined on the front
• As close to the horizontal as possible
• Head in natural alignment with the spine
• Water in line with the eyebrows or the hair line depending on the swimmer's buoyancy

Leg action:
• Long, almost straight leg movements
• Alternating up and down action
• Big toes usually pass close to each other
• Usually 'in toeing' (feet turning inwards) occurs to provide maximum effect
• Down kick starts at the hips and travels along through a slightly bent, but vigorously extending, knee to fully-stretched ankles and toes
• Down kick ends at about body thickness depth, that is about 30 to 35 cms
• Up kick starts at the hips, legs remain straight, ankles and toes fully extended
• Up kick ends just as heels break the surface
• Emphasis on the down kick

Arm action:
Propulsion
• Entry of hands, thumb/fingers before rest of hand and arm
• Entry of hands, elbow slightly bent, somewhere between a point opposite the shoulder and in line with the nose

• 'Catch' (point where the hand comes into firm contact with the water) occurs at a depth of between 15 and 20 cms
• Pull follows catch position, with the wrist remaining firm, fingers stretched. The hand travels slightly outwards then in a downwards and backwards movement close to and under the body and along its centre line. Elbow is bent in a 90 ° angle for a powerful, efficient action
• Push begins as hand passes a point below and level with the shoulder. The hand continues along the centre line but begins to return to its own side as it stretches back, palm still facing backwards, alongside the thigh prior to exit

Recovery
• Wrist rotates so the palm is facing the thigh
• Exit point close to the thigh
• Arm slightly bent with little finger uppermost, elbow leading the exit
• Movement is relaxed and over the water
• Arm passes as close to the ear as the swimmer's shoulder - mobility will allow
• Arm stretches forward for next entry

Breathing:
• To the side (usually swimmer's choice)
• Occurs once every complete arm cycle, that is when both arms have completed their action. This is known as unilateral breathing. Many competitive swimmers use bilateral breathing, which is breathing on alternate sides every one and a half arm cycles
• Usually of the 'explosive' type, that is a vigorous exhalation which commences just before the mouth is about to break the surface. The final driving-out of the air is immediately followed by a vigorous inhalation prior to the face returning to the downwards position. Another type of breathing is known as 'trickle' breathing, where the air is exhaled more slowly over a longer period of time.

Front Crawl

1. Right hand moving to catch point.

2. Right hand in pull phase.

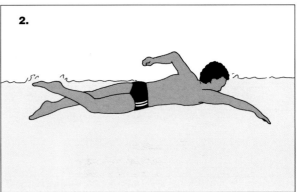

3. Right hand going into push phase.

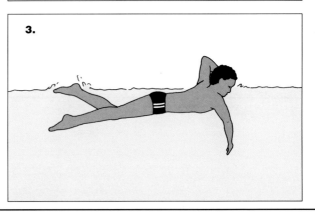

4. Right hand continuing push phase.

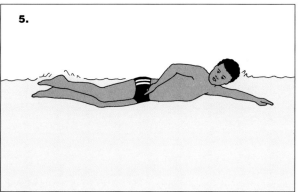

5. Relationship of breathing and end of push phase.

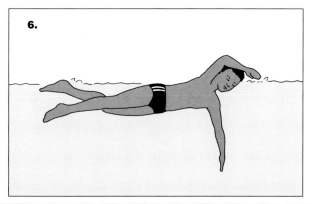

6. Right arm recovery forwards to entry position.

Timing/Coordination:
• Breathing usually occurs towards the end of the push phase of the arm action on the breathing side, just as the arm is about to commence its recovery
• The leading hand enters the water as the other hand is part way through its propulsive (push) phase
• The most common coordination of legs and arms is six leg beats to one complete arm cycle. Variations on this will be influenced by the experience and quality of the swimmer concerned

Coaching the Front Crawl
Make use of the whole-part-whole method of learning by allowing the swimmer to try out as much of the whole stroke as he can. It might not be a pretty sight, but at least both the coach and the swimmer will have a better understanding of the problems they are up against!

Some selected coaching practices
(with suggested coaching points)
• Push and glide actions with and without a float in order to improve body position.
('Stretch from fingers to toes'; 'try to squeeze your ears with the top of your arms')
• As above but introduce the leg action before the glide fades away.
('Try to keep your knees straight'; 'stretch your ankles and point your toes')
• Breathing practices standing in the shallow end or whilst trying the practices described above.
('Blow out fast and hard'; 'suck air in quickly'; 'try turning your head to the side to breathe')
• Arm action standing in shallow water or whilst attempting leg kick with no breathing action at this stage.
('Turn your head as your leading hand goes into the water'; 'remember to blow hard when breathing out')
• Introduce occasional breathing with arm actions over a width.
('Breathe once/twice/etc during the width'; 'look sideways as you turn your head to breathe'; 'breathe as your leading hand enters the water')

Coaching Front Crawl Turns

The most commonly-used turn in competitive front crawl swimming is known as the 'tumble'. There are several versions, but the principle is that as the swimmer approaches the wall his head is thrust downwards to perform a somersaulting movement with a half twist. This movement enables him to plant his feet on the wall, with the knees slightly bent, to make a vigorous drive away into full stretch and glide action. During the gliding action away from the wall the swimmer twists or rotates his body longitudinally back on to his front to return to the correct swimming position on surfacing.

Mushroom float

Some selected coaching practices

• Practise the 'mushroom' or tucked floating position.
• Standing in shallow water, practise forward-somersaulting activities.
• Push and glide movements under the surface.
• Standing in shallow water about one metre from and facing the wall, practise a somersaulting movement (with no twisting action) to plant the feet on the wall.
• Repeat previous practice but instead of standing, swim in to the wall from about two metres out. As the head drives down, the trailing hand should stay where it is alongside the thigh and the leading hand should complete its movement by coming alongside its thigh. At this point both hands are rotated so that the palms are pressed downwards. This will increase the speed of rotation in the somersault considerably.
• Repeat previous practice, but after planting feet on the wall, push off vigorously in a full stretch glide position on the back.
• Repeat previous practice, but during the push-off and glide start to twist onto the front to achieve the correct swimming position.
• Repeat as above, but try to introduce the twisting action into the latter part of somersaulting movement.

The above set practices will serve as a useful introduction to the front crawl tumble turn. Remember these practices should be taught in a progressive fashion and should take into consideration the confidence and swimming ability of the swimmer. You must also allow time for a large number of attempts at the various exercises, with appropriate feedback from the coach.

Note
With all but the first exercise, check the depth of the water for safety to avoid head injury.

For Front Crawl Starts see Head-first Entries in Chapter 6.

Front Crawl Turns

1. Approaching the wall the head drives down.

2. The hips move above the head as the somersault action starts.

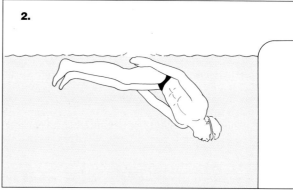

3. Hand movements assist the somersault action.

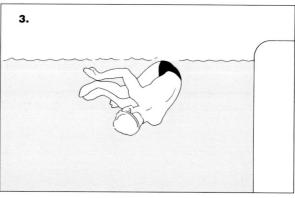

4. Feet ready to plant on the wall.

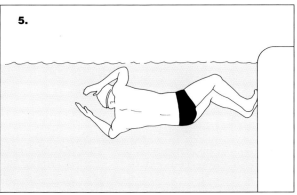

5. The drive from the wall begins.

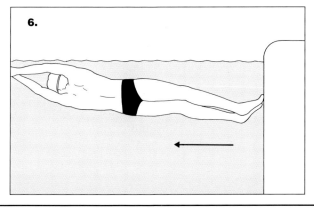

6. The drive from the wall in full stretch,

2. Back Crawl

This stroke has many of the characteristics of the front crawl except, of course, it is done on the back! The body is streamlined and horizontal , although not as streamlined as in the front crawl. There is a very slight lowering of the hips to facilitate the leg kick remaining in the water. This stroke too, is an alternating stroke. The arm action is less efficient because the shoulder muscles cannot be used to their full advantage whilst the body is on the back.

Body position:
• Streamlined on the back
• As close to the horizontal as possible
• Hips just lightly lower than the surface
• Head in natural alignment with the spine with the back of the head resting on the water and the chin in

Leg action:
• Long, almost straight leg movements
• Alternating up and down action
• Big toes usually pass close to each other
• Usually 'in toeing' (feet turning inwards) occurs to provide maximum propulsion
• Up kick starts at the hips and travels along through a slightly bent, but vigorously extending, knee to fully stretched ankles and toes
• Up kick ends just as toes break the surface
• Emphasis on the up kick
• Down kick starts at the hips, legs remain straight, ankles and toes fully extended
• Down kick ends at about body thickness depth, that is at about 30 to 35 cms

Arm action:
There are two types of arm action in this stroke, the 'straight arm' and 'bent arm' ('S' pull). Competitive swimmers almost invariably

use the bent arm action. When introducing the stroke, allow the swimmer to make use of the one that seems to come most easily. If the bent arm action can be developed, then it might avoid relearning at a later stage. However, the important point is that the swimmer gains the experience of learning to swim on his back.

Bent arm ('S' Pull):

Propulsion
- Entry of hands little finger first, thumb uppermost
- Arm straight, somewhere between a point opposite the shoulder and in line with the nose, depending on the mobility of the swimmer's shoulder joint
- Catch occurs at a depth of 15 to 20 cms
- Pull follows catch position, wrist remains firm, fingers initially stretched with downwards and outwards movement. The elbow begins to bend and the hand comes closer to the body, fingers moving upwards, palms facing towards the feet, and nearer to the surface of the water
- Push is directly backwards and begins as the hand passes a point level with the shoulder. At this point the bend at the elbow should be at about 90 °. The arm continues along a path parallel to the body centre line but gradually moving closer to the body as it makes a final accelerating thrust downwards past the hip
- The hand then moves back up towards exit point

Straight arm action:

Propulsion
- Entry of hands, little finger first with the thumb uppermost
- Arm straight, somewhere between a point opposite the shoulder and in line with the nose, depending on the mobility of the swimmer's shoulder joint
- Catch occurs at a depth of between 15 and 20 cms
- Pull follows from catch position, with the wrist firm and the arm straight and moving outwards and backwards in a semi-circular movement just under the surface. The fingers are stretched outwards, thumb uppermost
- Push begins as hand passes a point level with the shoulder. The arm continues its semi-circular path moving closer to the body and finishing at the thigh ready for exit point

Back Crawl

1. The right hand moving through catch.

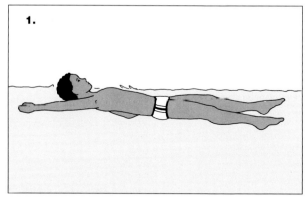

2. The right hand begins the pull phase.

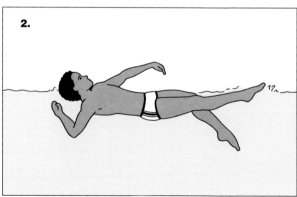

3. The right hand moving through the push phase.

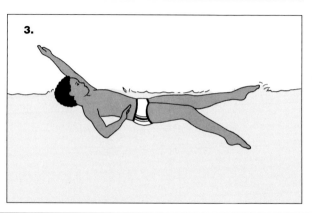

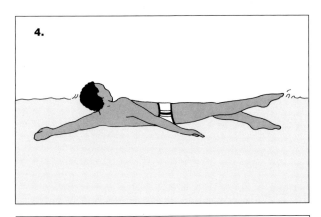

4. 4. The right hand travels towards the exit point.

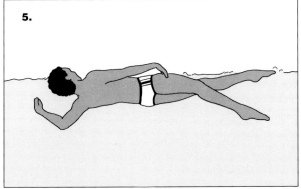

5. 5. Right hand beginning recovery.

6. 6. Right hand recovering over the water towards entry point.

Recovery (both arm actions)
• Exit point close to the thigh
• Arm straight (if exit was thumb-first then arm rotates during recovery for little-finger entry)
• Arm passes as close to the ear as the swimmer's shoulder mobility will allow
• Arm reaches ahead of the swimmer for next entry

Breathing:
• This is usually related to the hand entry (see below)

Timing/Coordination:
• As one hand enters there is an out-breath, followed by an in-breath as the other hand enters
• The stroke should be a continuous windmilling action so that, as the leading hand enters the water, the other hand is completing its propulsive phase
• The most common coordination of legs and arms is six leg beats to complete one arm cycle. Any variation in this will be influenced by the experience and quality of the swimmer concerned

Coaching the Back Crawl
Some selected coaching practices
(with suggested coaching points)
• Floats are more effectively used whilst on the back if they are held over the thighs. In the early stages 'cuddling' a float over the chest or holding one under each arm and letting them go whilst swimming, is often effective
('Tummy up'; 'look up at the ceiling'; 'chin in';'stretch the legs'; 'keep the knees straight','kick the legs, scull with the hands';'kick the legs, scull with the hands then start the proper arm action';'pull/lift-out with the arms')
• Use some of the front crawl practices and coaching points but perform them on the back.

Back Crawl Turns
1. The touch
2. Head goes back and knees lift.
3. The spinning movement brings the feet to the wall.
4. A vigorous drive and stretch away.

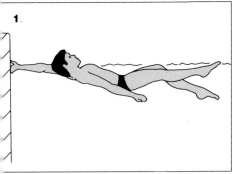

1.

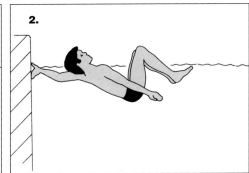

2.

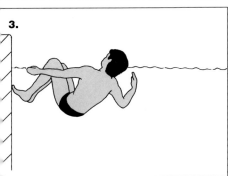

3.

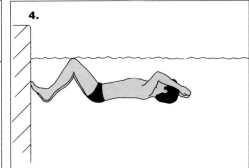

4.

Coaching Back Crawl Turns

A commonly-used turn in competitive back crawl swimming is the 'pivot' or 'spin'. As the swimmer approaches the wall the head drops backwards, the leading hand touches and initiates the tucked 'spin' or 'pivoting' movement bringing the feet round to plant on the wall, with the knees bent, to make a vigorous drive away into the full stretch and glide action.

Some selected coaching practices
• Practise a tucked floating position on the back.
• As above, but use the hands to paddle in a spinning movement in either direction.

Note

As with front crawl turns, work on the back crawl turn should be taken progressively with lots of feedback from the coach.

• Practise push and gliding movements on the back under the surface.

• Lie on the back in the water with the head back and towards the wall and an arm's length away. Reach for the wall, fingers pointing downwards, using the touch to initiate the spin towards the leading hand. Knees should be tucked ready for the feet to be planted firmly on the wall in a stretched position for a vigorous push off.

• As previous practice but swim into the wall from about two metres out.

• Repeat previous practice, but after planting feet on the wall push off vigorously in a full stretch glide position on the back, with legs and arms fully extended.

• Repeat previous practice, but during the glide, the leg kick begins in readiness for the start of the full stroke.

Back Crawl Starts

1.'Take your marks'

• Swimmer is in the water in a curled position facing the wall with hands grasping the edge. Both feet are firmly planted on the wall and the foot position is usually is 'staggered' with one foot at a slightly higher level than the other. The chin should be close to the wall.

2. 'Go'

• The head goes up and back and the arms sweep vigorously upwards, round and backwards above the water surface.

• Swimmer explodes upwards and backwards with the legs, pushing the hips up, in a vigorous thrust away from the wall.

• The above actions, if performed properly, will cause the body to stretch and arch in a back dive-like action above the water with the arms fully extended above the head, and the head back to ensure that the hands enter the water before the rest of the body.

• The above movements are followed by a fully-stretched glide action in the water which is ended as the full stroke is introduced.

Back Crawl Starts

The swimmer explodes upwards and backwards.

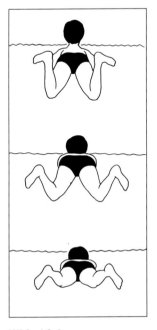

Whip kick
The drive is mainly
backwards.

3. Breaststroke

This stroke is the least efficient of the strokes as not only does the leg action cause it to be swum in something less than the horizontal, but the arm recovery is made under water. It is what is known as a 'simultaneous' stroke and is often used by recreational swimmers who simply want to move steadily through the water, looking where they are going. There are two types of leg kick and two types of arm action. The descriptions below relate the appropriate arm to leg movements in bracketed notes.

Body position:
• Streamlined on the front
• Close to the horizontal, bearing in mind the constraints of the leg action
• Hips just below the water surface
• Head position will vary during the stroke cycle
• Shoulders parallel to the surface of the water

Leg action:
There are two types of leg action in this stroke, the 'whip kick' and the 'wedge kick'. Competitive swimmers almost invariably use the whip kick. When introducing the stroke to a swimmer for the first time, allow him to use the one that seems to come most easily. If the whip action can be developed first it might avoid re-learning at a later stage. However, the important point is that the swimmer experiences the simultaneous action of the legs.

Whip kick:
(relates to Bent Arm Action, page 70)
• Commences from the fully extended position in which the legs are straight and together and the ankles and feet are stretched
• Movements are performed simultaneously by both legs

• Knees bend and begin to spread in recovery, smoothly bringing the heels, with the toes still pointing backwards, towards the buttocks. The spread of the knee and heel in recovery should be at hip width or just a little wider. There should be no excessive flexion at the hip: the emphasis should be on raising the heels upwards and forwards towards the buttocks

• The propulsive phase is a smooth transfer from the recovery and begins as the heels reach their closest point to the buttocks; the feet begin to turn out (evert) with the ankles flexed (dorsi-flexed)

• With the feet still everted and dorsi-flexed the accelerating legs sweep vigorously back, downwards and slightly out until they are fully extended. During the movement the feet should stay within the width of the shoulders

• As the legs reach the fully-extended position the ankles rotate so the feet are extended, or even pointing inwards (inverted), and the legs come together in readiness for the next recovery phase

Wedge kick:
(relates to Straight Arm Action, page 70)
• Commences from the fully-extended position in which the legs are straight and together and the ankles and feet are stretched
• Movements are performed simultaneously
• Knees bend and begin to spread and drop forward in recovery, with the heels remaining close together and the toes beginning to point outwards as they are drawn towards the buttocks. The knee spread in recovery, particularly if viewed from behind, will look wider than hip width as the thigh is brought well forward and the hip flexion is greater than in the whip kick
• The propulsive phase is a smooth transfer from the recovery and begins as the heels are almost together and reach their closest point to the buttocks. With the feet turned out (everted) and ankles flexed (dorsi flexed), the legs drive out wide and backwards, then move inwards in a continuous movement to come together
• Legs come together, toes and ankles extended, in readiness for the next recovery phase

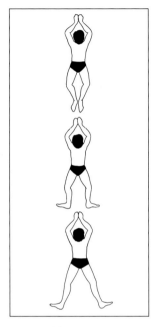

Wedge kick
The drive is outwards and backwards.

Note
Coaches are reminded that the breast-stroke kick can frequently produce painful, and often serious, knee conditions resulting from the joint attempting to rotate under excessive stress - not part of its original design specification! Be on the alert for this condition.

Arm action:

There are two types of arm action in this stroke, the 'straight arm' and 'bent arm'. Competitive swimmers almost invariably use the bent arm action. When introducing the stroke to a swimmer, allow him to use the one that seems to come most easily. If the bent arm action can be developed, then it might avoid re-learning at a later stage. However, once again, the important point is that the swimmer experiences simultaneous arm actions.

Bent arm:
(relates to the Whip Kick, page 68)
• Commences from fully-extended position ahead of the body, with hands close together and the fingers stretched, about 15 cms below the surface
• Arms move simultaneously outwards with the fingers still stretched, the palms facing backwards and the elbows high.
• As the catch is made, at about 15 to 20 cms depth just wide of the shoulder width, the elbows begin to bend as the hands move into the propulsive phase pulling downwards and backwards
• The pulling movement continues, with elbows still higher than the hands, until the arms are at their deepest point and almost level with the shoulders. From here they begin an accelerating circling action, bringing the hands close together under the chest into the recovery
• Recovery brings the hands forward, still close together, from under the chest to the fully-extended position ahead of the body once again

Straight arm:
(relates to the Wedge Kick, page 69)
• Commences from fully-extended position ahead of the body, with hands close together and the fingers stretched, about 15 cms below the surface
• Arms move simultaneously downwards, backwards and outwards with the fingers still stretched, palms facing backwards, and the arms straight. The catch is made at a depth of about 15 to 20 cms and the hands continue to move into the propulsive phase by pulling down, out and backwards

• The pulling movement continues, still with straight arms, until the hands are at their deepest point. Here the arms should be wider than shoulder width apart and at a 45 ° angle with the chest so that they can be kept in view by the swimmer without him turning his head. At this point they begin an accelerating, circling motion bringing the elbows in towards the chest wall and the hands close together under the chest into the recovery

• Recovery brings the hands forward, still close together, from under the chest back to the fully-extended position ahead of the body

Breathing:

For the Wedge kick/Straight arm stroke

If the swimmer is using the wedge kick/straight arm action for recreational swimming purposes, it is likely that the head will be up and breathing will not be a problem. A breath will probably be taken in the glide position (see Timing/Coordination below) above the surface because the head will be upright. The swimmer might benefit from being encouraged by the coach to exhale vigorously part-way through the arm pull, perhaps when the mouth is in the water. By having to lower the head just a little, any tension that might have built up in the neck muscles might also be released. Encouraging this practice will also pave the way for an introduction to the breathing action for the Whip kick/Bent arm action should the swimmer wish to pursue it later.

For the Whip kick/Bent arm stroke:

• Head is face down with the water at about eyebrow level whilst the arms are moving from the fully-extended position ahead of the body to the latter part of the pull phase

• As the pull phase moves into the circling action which starts the recovery, vigorous exhalation takes place so that, when the head is lifted, exhalation has only to be completed before rapid inhalation occurs

• The above movement will be accompanied by the raising of the shoulders upwards and forwards

Breaststroke (Whip kick)

1. Arms in full stretch positions, legs completing their drive.

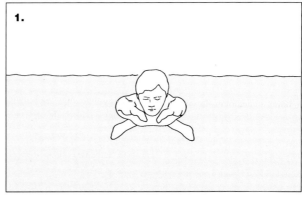

2. Hands at their deepest point with the elbows high.

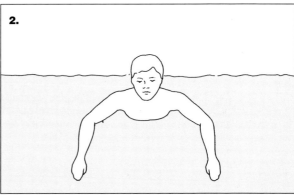

3. Elbows still high with the hands moving in under the body. Legs begin recovery.

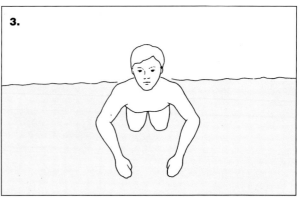

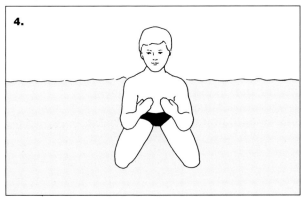

4. Hands in swirling recovery phase. Legs continue recovery.

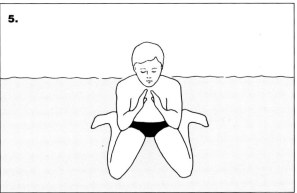

5. An alternative swirling hand-recovery position.

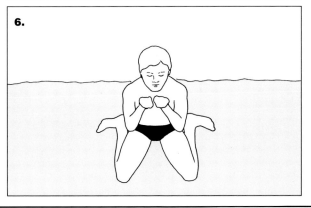

6. Elbows close in, hands stretching forwards in recovery. Legs driving vigorously backwards.

Timing/Coordination:

There are several variations, but basically two need to be considered. One is with a glide, for the recreational use of the stroke, the other without a glide, used by the competitive swimmer.

With a glide (usually recreational use):
• The arm pull begins from the full-stretch glide position
• The legs commence recovery ready to repeat the drive forward as the arms complete their pulling action and go forward to the breathing and gliding position
• The glide position is held momentarily as the legs and arms are at full stretch, prior to the arm action starting again

Without a glide (usually competitive use):
• From full-stretch position the arms pull
• As arm pull is being transformed into the swirling action prior to their recovery, breathing takes place as described above
• Near the completion of the arm recovery the legs commence the kick
• Arms are held forward until the leg kick is complete and then the sequence starts again

Coaching the Breaststroke

Some selected coaching practices
(with suggested coaching points)
• Legs-only actions will emphasize the need to turn the feet out as they drive backwards. Since the stroke is a simultaneous action this should also be highlighted together with the idea that the legs should be symmetrical in their movement. Whilst symmetry is not in the law of the stroke it is a point to work towards.
('Turn the feet out'; 'point the toes east and west'; 'bring your heels close to the seat'; 'draw circles with your heels'; 'try to kick with your legs behind you'; 'stretch your ankles as your legs come together')
• It often helps the swimmer, if he is having difficulty with the breaststroke kick, to practise it on his back so he can see what is going wrong. Use the same coaching points used when the swimmer was on his breast.

• Arm actions can be tried out in the full stroke or while standing in shallow water and leaning forward to try and attain the normal swimming position. If you intend the action to be practised in a stationary position, then suggest that the swimmer stands with the feet staggered to provide a more stable base. Sometimes it is worth encouraging the swimmer to walk forward, still with the upper body well forward and as close to the swimming position as possible.

('Press the arms back, down and round'; 'at the end of the push, swirl your hands round quickly and reach forward')

Some of the front crawl practices using push and glide activities both on front and back can be used here although, naturally, the coaching points will be different

Coaching Breaststroke Turns

The turn used in competitive breaststroke swimming is governed very strictly by the laws. The touch must be simultaneous, but it can be made at any level providing the shoulders remain horizontal. There are several other complexities in the laws governing this stroke which should be checked in the current *ASA Handbook*. For the coaching to be accurate, however, after each turn the swimmer should have only one complete arm cycle and one complete leg action whilst under water. The approach to the wall should happen at speed with the arms reaching forward. As contact is made the arms will bend, the head will come in close and the shoulder on the turning side will drop. The hands will push vigorously off the wall and the swimmer's body will rotate with bent knees in readiness for planting the feet on the wall. As the legs reach for the wall the arms should stretch forward under the water so that the vigorous leg drive from the wall coincides with the full stretching and gliding position. As the full effect of the glide is about to end, the arms and the legs begin their underwater action of the stroke.

Some selected coaching practices
• Vigorous push and gliding movements under the surface.
• Stand facing the wall an arm's length away. Jump for the wall, fingers pointing towards the turning side, using the touch to push

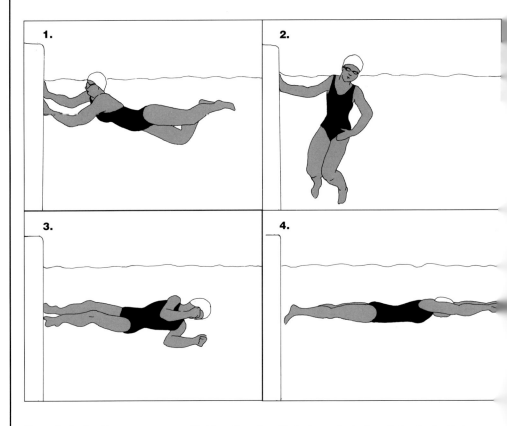

1.

2.

3.

4.

Breaststroke Turns
The first touch must be simultaneous with the shoulders horizontal. The body must be on the breast when the feet leave the wall.

For Breaststroke Starts see Head-first Entries in Chapter 6.

and initiate the spin with the knees tucked ready for the feet to be planted firmly on the wall.

• Repeat previous practice but swim into the wall from about three metres out.

• Repeat previous practice but, after planting feet on the wall, push off vigorously in a full-stretch glide position, with the arms and legs fully extended, on the front.

4. Butterfly

Developed in the early 1930s, this is the youngest of the swimming strokes. The swimming laws at the time failed to define the recovery phase in the breaststroke, with the result that some authorities argued that the spirit of the law meant it to be an underwater recovery, while others pointed out that, since the law offered no definition, the arms could be recovered above the surface. Out of this rather unpromising start the butterfly stroke was born. It was originally known as the butterfly breaststroke, but became known as the butterfly when it was recognized as a stroke in its own right in the 1950s. Like the breaststroke, it is a simultaneous stroke but, nowadays, with the legs moving up and down and the body moving in an undulating manner. Breaststroke leg actions are still permissible in the law but swimmers seldom, if ever, use them, preferring to use the more efficient, undulating, Dolphin kick. The stroke is now, in fact, second only to front crawl in speed.

Body position:
• Streamlined on the front
• As close to the horizontal as the leg action allows
• Hip level varies, according to the point in the stroke cycle, from being at the surface to about body thickness deep, hence its description as ' undulating'
• Head position generally in natural alignment with the spine, but again it varies according to point in the stroke cycle

Leg action:
The leg action of the Dolphin kick is known as a two-beat kick because there are two up kicks and two down kicks to one complete arm cycle. These kicks are often referred to as the 'major, minor' with the first downbeat seeming the stronger of the actions.
• Long, almost straight leg movements
• Simultaneous up and down action
• Knees are spread slightly at the beginning of the downkick
• Usually in-toeing (feet turning inwards) occurs towards the end of the down kick

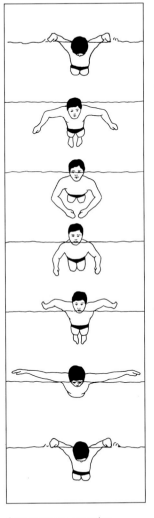

Arm recovery over the surface.

• Down kick starts at the hips and travels along through a slightly bent, but vigorously extending, knee to fully -stretched ankles and toes. This vigorous movement is both propulsive and causes the hips to rise
• Down kick ends at depth of about 50 to 60 cms
• Up kick starts at the hips while the lower legs are still extending on the down kick. Legs remain straight on the upward movement although the knees will bend as the hips initiate the next downward action. The result of the upkick will be to lower the hips
• Up kick ends as the toes come to the surface

Arm action:
Propulsion
• Entry of hands is simultaneous, thumb/fingers before the rest of the hand and arm
• Entry of hands with the elbows slightly bent, somewhere at a point opposite the shoulder or just outside it
• The catch occurs at a depth of about 15 to 20 cms with the hands pressing outwards and backwards and the elbows high in the water
• The pull follows the catch with the wrist remaining firm and the fingers stretched in circular outwards, downwards and backwards movement. The elbows remain high and the hands move to a point directly below them
• The push begins as the hands pass a point level with the shoulder. Keeping the elbows bent and the palms facing backwards, the hands accelerate backwards and in towards the body so that the thumbs come close together. The hands continue to push backwards and then move outwards along the thighs, extending the elbows, prior to exit

Recovery:
• Exit point is close to the thigh
• Arms are slightly bent as the elbows lead the exit, little finger uppermost
• Movement is a fast, relaxed, sideways and forwards swing clear of the water
• Arms stretch forward for the next entry

Breathing:
• To the front with the chin stretching forwards
• Occurs usually once every two complete arm cycles
• Usually of the explosive type: that is, a vigorous exhalation which commences just before the mouth is about to break the surface. The final driving-out of the air is then immediately followed by a vigorous inhalation prior to the face returning to the downwards position

Timing/Coordination:
• Breathing is usually on every second arm cycle
• Breathing usually begins towards the end of the push phase of the arm action, just as the arms are about to commence the recovery
• Breathing usually ends as the head is returning to the water with the hands reaching forward for entry
• The most common coordination of legs and arms is for the legs to make their major drive down as the hands enter and move through the catch into the pull phase. The second kick occurs as the hands move through the final stages of the push phase into the exit

Some selected coaching practices
(with suggested coaching points)
• Some of the front crawl practices using push and glide activities both on front and back can be used here although, naturally, the coaching points will be different.
• Legs-only actions should emphasize the vigorous down drive. Underline the simultaneous nature of the stroke and the demands of the laws. Often the leg kick is introduced to the swimmer by practising it with breaststroke arm actions which makes it easier to concentrate on leg movements.
('Stretch the ankles'; 'kick down hard';'keep the legs straight on the way up')
• Arm actions can be tried out in the full stroke or while standing in shallow water with the swimmer leaning forward to attain the swimming position as closely as possible. If the exercise is to be done in a stationary position then the feet should be staggered to provide a more stable base. Sometimes it is worth encouraging

Coordination of breathing and arm action.

the swimmer to walk forward, still with the upper body well forward and as close to the swimming position as possible.
('Press back, down and round'; 'at the end of the push stretch your elbows';'little finger out of the water first, elbows bent';'keep the hands and arms clear of the water on the way forward';'stretch for entry')
• Breathing is introduced firstly by not doing it at all over short distances, then by trying one exhalation/inhalation and building it up over a width or so. It can also be used in any of the arm practices shown above, which will link it in with the leg action.
('Kick down as your hands enter, kick down as your hands leave','blow out just before your hands leave, suck in as your arms recover';'let your chin lead your breathing';'reach forward with your chin')

For coaching practices for Butterfly Turns see pages 75-6, and for Butterfly Starts see Head-first Entries, Chapter 6.

Coaching Butterfly Turns

The turn used in competitive butterfly swimming is governed by laws very similar to those of the breaststroke. However, there is a difference in the technique of the underwater part of the turn in that the underwater push and glide in the breaststroke is deeper than that of the butterfly. In the butterfly the swimmer is allowed more than one leg kick underwater despite the fact that only one complete arm pull is permissible.

Butterfly

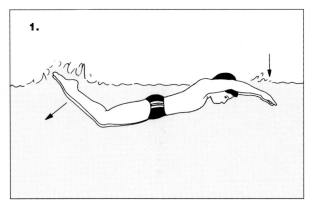

1. First downkick occurs as hands enter.

2. Vigorous arm pull as downkick is completed.

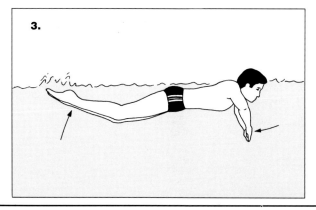

3. Pull phase ends and upkick commences.

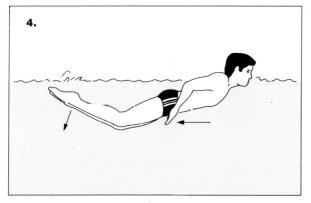

4. Push phase almost complete. Second downkick occurs.

5. Hands exit, second downkick completed.

6. Arms recover. Second upkick occurs.

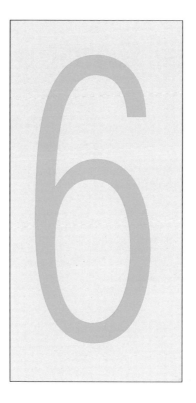

HEAD-FIRST ENTRIES

Head-first Entries

This section is deliberately entitled 'head-first' entries rather than diving. The term 'diving' implies steep and vertical entries into the water, and these require deep water. Even diving from the poolside requires a depth of more than the full stretch height (fingers to toes) of the diver, no matter how small and light in stature he might be.

This section, therefore, is designed to assist the coach in introducing head-first entries safely and developing them up to the plunge dive stage, which includes the correct practice for the start of front crawl, breaststroke and butterfly strokes. Remember ALL HEAD-FIRST ENTRIES ARE POTENTIALLY HAZARDOUS! Injuries resulting from head-first entries are frequently very serious.

Step 1: Early Introductory Practices

These practices are designed to familiarize the learner with being under the water and consist of a series of progressions which should gradually increase his confidence to try a head-first entry.

With the swimmer in the shallow end of the pool, encourage him to try the following exercises over a period of time:

• Pushing and gliding in the full stretch position with the face in the water.
• As above, but push and glide under the surface.
• Blowing bubbles into the water.
• Practise sitting on the bottom of the shallow end of the pool.
• As above, but encourage the swimmer to open his eyes.
• As above, facing a partner to see how many fingers or hands he is holding up.
• Perform a 'mushroom' or tucked float, again with the eyes open.
• Picking up objects from the bottom of the shallow area.
• Pushing and gliding beneath an arch made by a partner, either standing with feet astride or resting an arm on the surface.

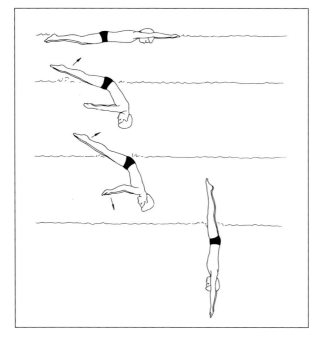

Head-first surface diving can be used as an early practice for head-first entries.

• Pushing and gliding through a hoop held by a partner.
• Handstanding on the bottom of the shallow area.
• Push and glide from the wall into a handstand.
• From standing in the shallow area, 'porpoise' dive head first to touch the bottom with the hands, into crouch position and then spring up to repeat.
• Head-first surface diving, that is, going down head first from swimming along the surface.
• Vigorous springing movements from the bottom of the shallow area to emphasize the powerful leg thrust.

Step 2 : Early Practices from the Poolside

The minimum depth of water for these practices should be at least one and a half metres. This requires the swimmer to be confident of his ability to be safe in at least that depth. Sometimes if the swimmer is neither tall nor heavy, the coach might feel that this depth of water is not necessary for him to make a safe head-first entry. This might well be true, but it should be remembered that if the swimmer should happen to make a steep entry by accident, he will not be experienced enough to cope with the ensuing rapid contact with the pool bottom. The result could be a very serious accident.

Feet-first entries making different shapes in the air.

Feet-first entries
• Stepping off the poolside into the water so the feet enter first.
• As above, but encourage the swimmer to make a tucked shape in the air, before stretching the legs to enter the water.
• Jumping from the poolside and stretching in the air before making a feet-first entry into the water.
• As above but tell him to make other shapes in the air, still with feet-first entries.
• As above, swinging the arms forwards and upwards to try to gain more height and stretch before entering the water feet first.

CAUTIONARY NOTE
With all entries from the poolside, whether they are feet or head first, careful attention should be paid to the position of the feet on the edge. These should be placed so that the toes are curled over the edge, gripping it firmly.

HEAD-FIRST ENTRIES

Sitting entry

Kneeling dive entry

Crouch dive entry

Step 3 : Head-first Entries

In the early stages of head-first entries the coach should encourage his swimmer to try for a flight which takes him away from the poolside and into the water hands/head first, with the remainder of the body following. Initially, steep entries should be discouraged. When the swimmer is ready and able to attempt this type of entry, the coach should ensure that there is an adequate, safe depth of water for his use.

• Sitting on the poolside, with heels on the rail or scum channel (can really only be done when one or other is available), ears between the upper arms and hands pointing outwards and downwards, the swimmer should gradually overbalance, lifting the hips to enter the water hands/head first without raising the head.

• **Kneeling dive** Starts with the front foot curled over the edge and the other knee on the poolside beside the front foot with the toes of the back foot curled under. Hands are stretched forward and down towards the water with the ears being squeezed between the upper arms. The body then rocks forward and as it overbalances the legs provide the drive taking it forwards, outwards and downwards, still with the head between the arms. Legs stretch on entry.

• **Crouch roll** Starting from the crouch position with the toes gripping the edge, hips high, arms reaching forwards and downwards and the upper arm squeezing the ears, the swimmer should gradually overbalance and roll into the water, hands/head first without raising the head.

• **Crouch dive** Starting as above, but as the hips overbalance the legs provide a vigorous drive forward, hands stretching for entry before the remainder of the body.

• **High crouch dive** Similar to the crouch dive above but with a more upright starting stance. The movement is started by the swimmer overbalancing which is followed by a vigorous leg drive to take the body forwards, outwards and downwards. The head remains between the upper arms with the hands reaching for the water. Legs remain stretched throughout the flight and entry.

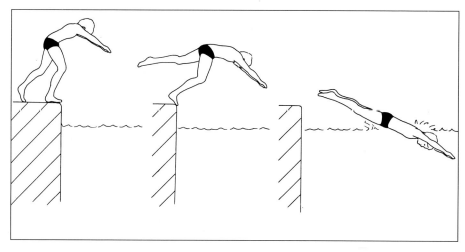

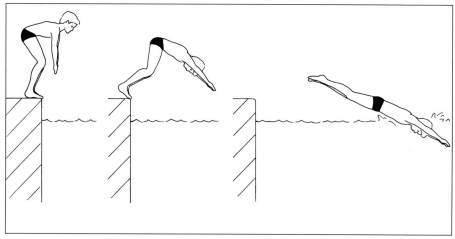

Top: Lunge dive
Bottom: Plunge dive

• **Lunge dive** Starts with swimmer positioned with one foot forwards and the toes gripping the edge, the other foot behind. Arms should be stretched forwards and downwards and the body bent forwards. The take-off is initiated by over balancing forwards followed by a vigorous drive with the legs. The hands reach forwards, outwards and downwards, the head remains between the upper arms and the whole of the body stretches forwards for entry.

• **Plunge dive** Starts in a position at the edge of the pool with the toes of both feet curled over the edge, knees slightly bent, body bent forward at the waist. The arms are either back or hanging downwards and the eyes should look forwards and downwards. The dive is initiated with an overbalancing movement forwards, followed by a vigorous swinging of the arms to achieve a full stretch position. This swing is combined with a powerful leg drive which brings about a full extension of the body from fingers to toes. The flight is outwards and downwards and at an angle of entry where the hands and head enter the water first. The angle should also be such that the momentum of the dive carries the body forward under the water: that is, the entry is streamlined and shallow rather than deep.

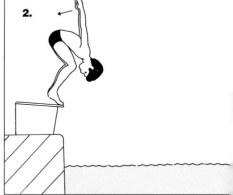

Wind-up start

Step 4 : Dive Starts

There are several types of dive starts used by competitive swimmers. However, because of the similarity to the plunge dive described in Step 3, this book will deal only with the 'wind-up' start.

Stance
(Taken up at the 'Take your marks' command)
Toes curled up firmly over the edge of the pool (or block), feet about hip-width apart, knees slightly bent, body bent forward with head in natural alignment with the spine in a comfortable position. The arms are forward at a point about halfway between the vertical and horizontal position, with the elbows relaxed and palms facing the water. The general weight of the body should be forward, rather than back.

Overbalance
(Initiated at the 'Go' command)
The general weight of the body moves slightly backwards before reacting in a rocking movement, bringing the centre of gravity in front of the feet. As this happens the arms begin a powerful circular movement upwards, backwards and round bringing them past the hips on their way forwards.

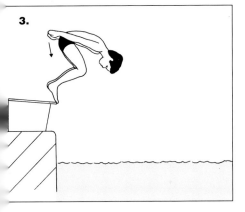

Flight
As the hands swing forward the whole of the body extends in a massively powerful movement which culminates in a vigorous drive from the legs, with the body fully extended in flight and the arms pointing forwards and downwards. During the early part of the flight the head is up, but it is lowered so that the ears are between the arms prior to entry.

Entry
The lowering of the head will cause a slight rotation of the body so that entry occurs with fingers/hands and head before the remainder of the body. The full extension is held in flight, and on entry is maintained under water in the glide.

Stroke variations

The angle of entry will be influenced by the stroke being swum, as will the action taken just as the glide is about to lose its full momentum. Front crawl swimmers will have the shallowest entry-angle and will commence kicking their way back to the surface, while butterfly swimmers will enter a little deeper and will follow the glide with the leg kick and a vigorous arm pull. Breaststrokers will dive more deeply and follow the glide with one long powerful underwater arm pull and leg kick prior to surfacing. Coaches are urged to consult the current ASA laws for all the starts.

Summary

All head-first entries are potentially dangerous and great care must be taken in the teaching of them. Progress should be taken in stages along the following lines:

1. Introductory practices, which include exercises and games, to familiarize the swimmer with being under the water.
2. Early practices from the poolside - including feet-first entries.
3. Head-first entries from the sitting position progressing to the kneeling dive, crouch dive, high crouch dive, lunge dive and finally the plunge dive.
4. Dive starts should eventually be taught as reactions to the commands 'Take your marks' and 'Go' in readiness for competitive swimming.

CAUTIONARY NOTE

Practising dive starts in shallow water is DANGEROUS for those new to the skills. For these swimmers to practise from starting blocks in shallow water is even more dangerous. Coaches should be alert to the dangers of such practices. Furthermore, they should also be particularly vigilant when inexperienced swimmers perform dive starts under competition conditions, both in individual and relay events, and especially in pools which are not familiar to them.

FITNESS AND HEALTH

Fitness and Health

Coaches should be aware of the influence they can have over the attitudes of their swimmers to fitness and health. They should encourage them not only in the short term objective of getting fit for competition, but make them realize the value of exercise in their lifestyles. Coaches whose only consideration is fitness for competition, particularly for the young, have got the balance of their work wrong; remember, disenchantment with competition swimming might well lead to disenchantment with swimming or exercise in general. Do not swim the fun and enjoyment out of swimming.

Exercise

Swimming as an exercise makes a wide range of demands on the body. It requires extensive use of a large number of muscles, the flexibility of their associated joints and an increase in the work of the heart and lungs. Much will depend on an individual's age and general fitness when starting the sport as to the exact amount of work which can be done. As with most sports, done in moderation and assuming that an individual's state of health is generally good, the above demands should be within the capabilities of most people. Start the swimmer off gently and carefully to see how he copes. This applies particularly to the older swimmer who very often wants to relive the swimming splendour of his youth and goes for a new world record in his first three minutes in the water!

Coaches are urged to make the demands fit the individual, not the individual fit the demands. This may well involve protecting the individual from himself and his misconceptions about his current swimming capabilities.

Hygiene

Part of the training of a young swimmer is in the area of hygiene. The use of handkerchiefs and toilet and shower facilities is not only for the individual's own benefit, but for the community in general. The prevention of the spread of infection should be everybody's responsibility, and personal cleanliness makes an important contribution. One spin-off is that good habits will probably make an individual more socially acceptable, so peer pressure often works to good effect.

The swimming environment has high standards of hygiene and cleanliness and coaches should ensure that their swimmers live up to them.

First Aid for the Swimmer

Loss of consciousness, usually due to a head injury, is a common problem in sport and although in most cases the swimmer recovers completely, it is always a potential problem and should be treated very seriously. It is advisable for all trainers, coaches or swimmers involved in the sport to take a proper First Aid course. The use of artificial respiration and heart massage can save a life but to be effective must be carried out immediately, and cannot wait even a few minutes for professional help to arrive. The commonest cause of death in an unconscious person is an obstruction of the airway, and in most cases correct First Aid techniques can prevent this.

If the swimmer is breathing normally, he or she may be put into the recovery position which ensures that the mouth and nose remain clear if they vomit. If there has obviously been a serious neck injury and the person is still breathing normally, it is not advisable to move the head at all but watch the person's breathing all the time while you wait for professional help to arrive.

If the swimmer is not breathing or is breathing with difficulty (e.g. gargling, gasping or breathing irregularly), start expired air resuscitation (E.A.R.)

Expired Air Resuscitation (E.A.R.)
This is not difficult but is potentially very hazardous if you do not know exactly what to do. You need to practice the procedure, and

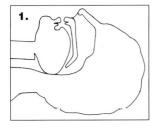 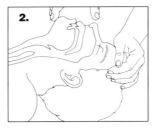 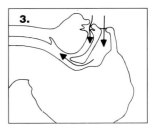

the only way to do this is on a dummy during a First Aid or RLSS course. Never try it on a healthy person.

The ABC of resuscitation :Airway, Breathing, Circulation.

Airway

Lie the swimmer on the back, lift the chin up, remove any obstruction in the mouth such as dentures, vomit, blood or broken teeth as far down as you can reach. This may be enough to start the person breathing again. If not, start mouth to mouth resuscitation.

Breathing

Keeping the chin up, pinch the nose and breathe out into the person's mouth at the same time as watching the chest which should expand. Take your mouth away and the person's chest falls, expelling the air while you take another breath yourself. Continue at your own breathing rate. After three or four breaths check that the person's heart is beating by feeling for a pulse at the side of the Adam's apple. If it is, continue mouth to mouth resuscitation until breathing begins or help arrives. If not, begin cardiac massage.

Circulation

If the heart has stopped, it is possible to pump blood around the body artificially by rhythmically squeezing it with hard pushes on the breast bone. This is called external chest compression (E.C.C.). When E.A.R. is combined with E.C.C. it is known as cardio-pulmonary resuscitation (C.P.R.). It is important that you go on a course and learn how to do it.

Clearing the Airway
The tongue of an unconscious person can fall to the back of the throat (1) and prevent the person from breathing. Raising the chin (2) lifts the tongue forwards and is often enough to free the airway (3).

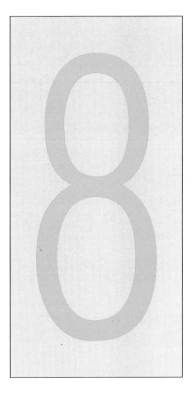

WHAT NEXT?

What Next?

No book of this size and nature can tell the coach all there is to know about good practice and the possible pitfalls. The important thing is to know where to turn for further information when it is needed. The following list is not exhaustive but will point the coach in the right direction.

1. Other reading

ASA *ASA Handbook,* ASA annual publication - see address below

ASA *Laws of the Sport* , ASA annual publication - see address below

ASA/Savlon *Babes in the Water,* ASA 1984

ASA *The Teaching of Swimming*, ASA 1987

Barr, D. & Gordon, A. *Water Polo*, Educational Productions 1980

Cross, R. (Editor) *The ASA Guide to Better Swimming*, Pan Books 1987

Elkington, H. & Chamberlain, J. *Synchronised Swimming*, David & Charles 1986

Gray, J. *Diving Instruction*, ASA 1978

Hardy, C. *Handbook for the Teacher of Swimming*, Pelham 1987

Harrison, J. *Anyone can swim*, The Crowood Press, 1987

Harrison J. (Editor) *Teaching of Swimming for those with Special Needs* , ASA 1986

National Coaching Foundation various coaching packs -see address below

Rackham G. *Diving Complete* , Faber and Faber 1975

Royal Life Saving Society *Life Saving*, Handbook published in eight separate parts -see address below

Sports Council and Health and Safety Commission *Safety in Swimming Pools* , Sports Council 1988 - see address below

2. Addresses

England

The Amateur Swimming
Association
Harold Fern House
Derby Square
Loughborough, LE11 OAL
Telephone: 0509 230431

National Coaching Foundation
4 College Close,
Beckett Park
Leeds LS6 3QH
Telephone: 0532 744802

Royal Life Saving Society UK,
Mountbatten House
Studley,
Warwickshire, B80 7NN
Telephone: 052 785 3943

Sports Council
16 Upper Woburn Place
London WC1
Telephone: 01 388 1277

Ireland and Northern Ireland

The Irish ASA
6 Maywood Crescent
Dublin 5
Telephone: 31 34 76

Scotland

The Scottish ASA
Airthrey Castle
University of Stirling
Stirling FK9 4LA
Telephone: 0786 70544

Wales

The Welsh ASA
National Sports Centre for
Wales
Sophia Gardens
Cardiff, CF1 9SW
Telephone: 0222 397571

WHAT NEXT?

Australia

Australian ASA
Suite 21a
56 Nerida Street
Chatswood
New South Wales 2067

RLSS Australia
PO Box 321
St Leonards
New South Wales 2065

Canada

Canadian ASA
333 River Road
Vanier City
Ontario

RLSS Canada
64 Charles Street East
Toronto M4Y 1T1

India

Swimming Federation of India
3552 Darwaja's Khancha
Shahpur
Ahriedabad
India 380 001

New Zealand

New Zealand ASA
PO Box 11-115
Wellington

RLSS New Zealand
264 Armagh Street
PO Box 13-489
Christchurch

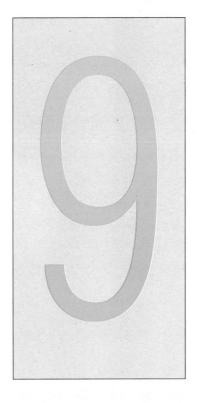

LAWS OF THE SPORT

LAWS OF THE SPORT

LAWS OF THE SPORT

THE FOLLOWING ARE SELECTED EXTRACTS FROM THE LAWS AS PUBLISHED IN THE ANNUAL *A.S.A. HANDBOOK* OR *LAWS OF THE SPORT*. BOTH ARE OBTAINABLE FROM THE A.S.A..

CONTENTS

EXPENSES

52. Expenses necessarily incurred for travelling, hotel and meals, may be offered to and accepted by a swimmer or official in the circumstances and not exceeding the scales set out below, provided that in no case shall the amount paid or reimbursed exceed the total sum actually expended.

52.1 Whoever pays expenses must be satisfied as to the reasonable accuracy of the claim. In case of expenditure subject to Value Added Tax, receipts, with this recorded, must be attached to the authorised Expense Form and produced to the official duly authorised by the Amateur Swimming Association or by the District in which the expenses or part of them were authorised or incurred.

52.2 Expenses may be paid only to an official or swimmer who takes part in an event under A.S.A.Laws.

52.3 Scale of permissible expenses:

52.3.1 *Rail.* Second class, or at the lowest prevailing fare. The sum payable for rail fares is from the point of departure to the venue of the event, and return to the home town.

52.3.2 *Steamer.* First class.

52.3.3 *Public Service Vehicle.* Actual fare. Taxi-cab fare when no cheaper means of transport is available.

Note: It is contrary to this law for a swimmer or official to receive a railway or other public service season ticket.

52.3.4 *Air.* The lowest prevailing rate; if an aircraft is especially chartered, the amount actually expended provided that when there is an air line operating, the lowest prevailing rate shall not be exceeded.

52.3.5 *Private Hire Motor Coach.* The amount actually expended in respect of persons entitled to expenses.

52.3.6 *Privately Owned Vehicle.* A swimmer or official using his own vehicle may receive payment at the rate of 12p per mile. The basis of calculation shall be mileage of the shortest route from the point of departure to the destination and return.

52.3.7 *Subsistence allowance.* Where a swimmer or official is necessarily absent from his home or place of work, subsistence and hotel allowance may be claimed and received subject to the following maxima (all of which are exclusive of VAT) and to the production of receipts, except when the expenditure on any one meal does not exceed £1.00.
Where the period of absence exceeds:
4 hours but does not exceed 6 hours - £2.50
6 hours but does not exceed 12 hours - £5.00

12 hours but does not exceed 24 hours - £7.50
24 hours - £7.50 for each complete period for 24 hours and as above for any remaining period.
Where hotel accommodation is necessarily occupied - £12.00 per night in addition to the above subsistence rates. Higher rates may be approved by the A.S.A. Committee or by a District Executive Committee in special circumstances.

Note: Where more than one venue is attended on the same day or during the same trip, the expenses must be pooled and apportioned. No duplication of expenses is permitted.

ADVERTISING

53. Advertising at Events Promoted by the A.S.A.

53.1 Technical Equipment, worn in the water.

53.1.1 Costumes - it is not permitted to wear any visible item in the form of advertising other than the trademark of the manufacturer not exceeding 16 sq cm in area.

53.1.2 Hats - may carry two advertisements, including that of manufacturer. These may be up to 16 sq cm in area each and may be two of manufacturer, or one of manufacturer and one of commercial sponsor.

53.2 Poolside Equipment

53. 2. 1 Towels and bags - may carry two advertisements as for hats above, up to 600 sq cm each in size, but letters may not exceed 10cm in height, and the actual name of manufacturer or commercial sponsor may not exceed 50 sq cm: Towels and bags supplied before 1st January 1989 are exempt from this ruling.

53.2.2 Tracksuits and Officials' Uniforms - may carry two advertisements on the top and two on the trousers or skirt, as for hats, and may not exceed 16 sq cm, each in area. The logo of the manfacturer or commercial sponsor may be repeated as well but the same name may be used only once on each article of clothing.

53.3 Body Advertisement This is not allowed in any way whatsoever.

53.4 General No slogans may be used in advertising, nor names of products involving tobacco or alcohol. In all cases of doubt, advertisements should be submitted to the Secretary of the A.S.A. for approval.

53.5 Referees at events organised under A.S.A. Laws shall control advertising.

GENERAL COMPETITION LAWS

101. Eligibility

101.1 A competitor is eligible to compete in competitions unless he has competitive swimming as his sole occupation or business on which he is financially dependent for living.

101.2 Any competitor eligible to compete shall be registered with the A.S.A. in accordance with Law 110.

101.3 An eligible competitor shall not compete against a person ineligible to compete except in Masters competitions, lifesaving competitions approved by the A.S.A., or when in the Services, and then only in Inter-Service competitions. Breach of this Law should be dealt with under the Judicial Laws.

102. Swimming and Trust Funds.
Any financial advantage accruing to a swimmer from his athletic fame or competitive results shall be paid into a swimming fund, or legally established trust fund, administered by the Hon. Treasurer of the A.S.A. who will also pay all legitimate claims from the fund.

103. Club Members.
The competing members of any club wishing to affiliate to a District must be eligible to compete as defined in

Law 101.1 except for those members competing in Masters competitions, and every affiiated club shall have a published rule to that effect.

104. Reinstatement. A person who is ineligible to compete may apply at any time to the District to which his club is affiliated, to be reinstated as an eligible competitor . The District may grant the application if it is satisfied that he complies with Law 101.1 and has not claimed the balance of his swimming or trust fund.

105. Competitions under A.S.A. Laws. All galas, contests and exhibitions held or sponsored by an affiliated body shall be held under A.S.A. Laws.

All advertisements, entry forms, programmes, tickets and official notices shall include the following words:

'Affiliated to the...(District)... Counties A.S.A.'
'Under A.S.A. Laws.'

106. Permits. An unaffiliated body or person wishing to sponsor a gala, contest or exhibition under A.S.A. Laws must obtain a permit from the District Hon. Secretary.

106.1 Application for the permit must be made on the official form and must be received by the District Hon. Secretary at least twenty-eight days before the event, accompanied by a fee of £3.15 or such smaller sum and the district may decide.

The application must state:-

106.1.1 The date, time and place of the meeting or event.

106.1.2 Full details of all events on the programme.

106.1.3 The guaranteed value of each prize.

106.1.4 The amount of entry fee for each event. The entry fee must include admission.

106.1.5 The date for the closing of entries.

106.1.6 An undertaking to comply with A.S.A. Laws.

106.1.7 If the meeting includes an open handicap event the name of the official handicapper.

106.2 A permit may be refused without a reason being stated.

106.3 Any gala, contest or exhibition for which a permit has been issued shall be held under A.S.A. Laws and all advertisements, entry forms, programmes, tickets and official notices shall include the following words:-

'By permit of the ... (District)... Counties A.S.A.'

'Under A.S.A. Laws.'

106.4 The permit shall be signed by the District Hon. Secretary and be available for inspection at the gala, contest or exhibition for which it was granted. A report of all permits issued or refused shall be made to the next meeting of the District Executive.

106.5 A permit shall not be granted :-

106.5.1 To a suspended swimmer,

106.5.2 to an individual, except where the meeting is in aid of a stated charity approved by the District, in which case a copy of the financial statement , duly audited, must be sent to the District Hon. Secretary within one month of the date of the meeting.

106.5.3 to a club eligible for affiliation which has previously been granted a permit

106.5.4 for a competition, contest or exhibition to be held in a place of public entertainment such as a theatre, music hall, circus, variety exhibition or any other form of mixed entertainment.

107. Galas held in another District. An affiliated body wishing to hold a gala, contest or exhibition outside the District to which it is affiliated shall obtain permission of its District and of the District in which

the event is to be held.

108.Gala Advertisements

108.1 A District Hon. Secretary may require the withdrawal of an advertisement which, in his opinion, is misleading or incorrect. He shall report such action to the next meeting of the District Executive.

108.2 A participant in a gala, contest or exhibition shall not be advertised under a misleading or incorrect title. The word 'champion' may only be used provided the championship title is also quoted, and the championship is one recognised by the A.S.A.

109. Right to Participate

109.1 Any competitor may join as many clubs as he wishes, but he is allowed to represent only one at a time.

109.2 No club shall prevent a member from belonging to another club or competing for another club. No person or club may promote or take part in an open competition which has a condition preventing a swimmer from competing because he is a member of more than one club.

109.3 Any competitor who temporarily or permanently changes his residence to another country may join a club affiliated to the respective Member in the new country.

109.4 Any competitor who wishes to represent a club in another country must make a written declaration of his intention to his former club and to the new club. The right to represent the new club may be allowed after a minimum of one month following the request.

110. Registration

110.1 All members of affiliated clubs, aged 10 years and over who enter National, District, County or Local Association Championships or Competitions, Open Meets or Leagues which culminate in a National fnal must register with the A.S.A. in accordance with regulations approved and published by the A.S.A. Committee.
Promoters of low level competitions and Open Meets which are restricted to a local area may apply to the A.S.A. for exemption of competitors for registration.
A member, when registering, must disclose the names of all clubs of which he is am member, with the dates from which his unbroken membership started Local Associations will be as determined by the Districts and notified to the Secretary of the A.S.A.

110.2 Members of clubs Not Affiliated to the A.S.A.

110.2.1 A member of a club which is affiliated to the Scottish or Welsh A.S.A. who enters open competition under A.S.A.laws in the name of that club shall be registered in Scotland or Wales.

110.2.2 A member of a club which is affiliated to any other national governing body which is affiliated to F.I.N.A. shall have a valid status certificate (see Law 133.1).

110.2.3 If a member of a club as set out in 110.2.1 or 110.2.2 wishes to compete in the name of a club affiliated to the A.S.A., or its Districts he must register with the A.S.A.

110.3 All Technical Officers in Swimming, Diving, Synchronised Swimming and Water Polo on District and A.S.A. Lists of Officials, together with all moderators, approved teachers and tutors of the Association's educational awards, all of whom shall be members of A.S.A., as defined in Law 3, shall register.

110.4 Each registered person will be given a Registration Number and a Registration Card bearing his name and number. The card must be produced at a competition on demand to an authorised official whenever the holder is competing and the number must be quoted on any document where it is required.

110.5 Registration fees, which may be different for various classes of registered persons shall be fixed by the A.S.A. Committee annually by the 31st July and shall take effect on 1st April following. They shall be notified to all clubs who already have registered members and shall be published in the Regulations for Registration in the A.S.A. Handbook. A person registering in more than one category shall pay only one fee which shall be in the category which has the highest fee.

110.6 Registration may be made and amended at any time during the year and shall be effective from the date on which a correct registration form and fee is received at A.S.A. Headquarters, and recorded by the Registrar.

110.7 All registrations shall lapse on 31st March each year unless renewed before that date.

111. Open Competitions

111.1 An open competition is a competition to which entry is not limited to members of any one club. A promoter may, however, impose other restrictions on entry. An inter-club contest is not regarded as an open competition if:

111.1.1 it involves not more than eight clubs, each of which has been individually invited by the promoter who has supplied the conditions, and

111.1.2 the whole event takes place in the pool on one occasion, and

111.1.3 the contest does not form part of a series of such events, the results of which are aggregated or considered together to decide the eventual winner, e.g. as in a league competition.

111.2 The promoter of an open competition may, at his discretion, refuse to accept any entry. If he does so he must, if requested by the entrant, give the reasons for his refusal in writing. An entry, having been accepted, may be returned at any time if it is found that the information given on the entry form is incorrect in a material particular.

111.3 Entry forms

Entrants to an open competition shall complete an entry form which must contain at least the following information:

111.3.1 Individual Events

111.3.1.1 The entrants registered name and registration number.

111.3.1.2 A declaration that he is an eligible competitor, unless the event is a Masters event open also to ineligible competitors.

111.3.1.3 A declaration that he accepts the promoter's conditions.

111.3.1.4 The name of an affiliated club of which he is a member in the name of which he wishes to compete and which has been included on his registration form.

111.3.2 Team Events

111.3.2.1 The name of the team.

111.3.2.2 A declaration by the team manager that:-
a) All the members from whom his team is to be selected are registered, and eligible to be members of the team.
b) he accepts on behalf of the team the promoter's conditions,
c) all members of his team comply with any age conditions.

111.3.2.3 A declaration signed by the team manager that the information given is correct.

111.3.3 Promoter's Conditions.
If the entry form does not state the promoter's conditions, they shall be made available by the promoter on request.

111.3.4 Incomplete or Inaccurate Information.
If the information required is not given fully or is found to be materially incorrect, the entry shall be void and the entry fee forfeited unless the information is completed or fully corrected by the closing date for entries.

111.4 Competitors. An entrant is regarded as a competitor in an event as soon as his entry has been accepted. He ceases to be a competitor if his entry is returned or he withdraws before the event is started.

111.5 Unregistered Swimmers in Open Team Competitions.
If, between the submission of an entry for an open team competition and the start of the competition, a team manager finds that, because of withdrawals of swimmers originally selected, he has insufficient registered members to complete his team, he may include unregistered members provided that:

111.5.1 they are otherwise eligible to compete,

111.5.2 the promoter and the referee are informed before the contest starts and given the names of the unregistered swimmers,

111.5.3 the team manager ensures that they are registered within 14 days. Such swimmers shall be permitted to swim in only one gala before being registered, but may be allowed to swim in up to 3 rounds of one competition without the production of his registration card. The promoter shall notify the Registrar of the names and clubs of the swimmers.

111.6 Exemptions from Registration. Open competitions under A.S.A. Laws which are promoted by any one of the following affiliated private associations and restricted to its own members shall be exempt from the requirement for the swimmers to be registered: The three Service Associations separately or in combination, The English Schools SA, its Divisions and area Associations, British Students Sports Federation
Air Training Corps
Army Cadet Force Association
The Boys' Brigade
British Blind Sport
The British Deaf Sports Council
British Long Distance Swimming Association
The British Polytechnics Sports Association
British Rail
British Sports Association for the Disabled

The Church Lads' and Church Girls' Brigade
The Civil Service A.S.A.
The Fire Service Sports and Athletic Association
The Girl Guides Association
The Independent Schools Association
Modern Pentathlon Association of Great Britain
Police Athletic Association
Scout Association
Sea Cadet Corps

District Associations may grant exemptions from registration to affiliated private associations connected with bodies not mainly concerned with swimming.

112. Unauthorised Relations

112.1 A member of an affiliated club may not compete wth or take part in a demonstration or exhibition with a swimmer who is not a member of a club affiliated to a District of the A.S.A., Scottish A.S.A., Welsh A.S.A., or to any F.I.N.A. member, other than provided for in Law 113.

112.2 Any swimmer who is or has been a member of any South African Sports Federation is not eligible to be a member of any F.I.N.A. Member or to compete in their competitions.

112.3 No affiliated club shall have any kind of swimming relationship with a body which is not affiliated to the A.S.A. or to F.I.N.A. or is suspended by them.

113. Private Associations. Members of Clubs which are units of a Private Association shall be exempted from the provisions of Law 112.1 in respect of competitions confined to the members of the Private Association.

114. Swim-Fit Programme. A District Association may grant dispensation from Law 112.1 where they are satisfied that the event in question forms part of a bona-fide Swim-Fit programme, subject to the payment of a special Membership Registration Fee not to exceed £50.00.

115. First Claim. When a swimmer is a member of more than one club taking part in a competition between clubs, the club of which he has been in longest unbroken membership on the day of the event shall have first claim on his services for this event.

115.1 Unless the rules governing a competition declare to the contrary, a competitor who is a member of more than one club may select the name of the club under which he enters an individual event.

115.2 Officers and men on the active list of the Royal Navy, Army, or Royal Air Force become first claim for their Service organisations upon joining the Service, but any person who has actually competed for his civilian club in a current competition at the time of joining the service, shall remain first claim for his civilian club for the purpose of that competition until its completion, except that should he be called upon to represent his Service in a representative Service team in any other competition, such call shall take precedence over all other claims.

115.3 For School swimmers, in general the school should have priority, but where an individual swimmer is following a serious routine of training under his club coach, and is being prepared for District and National Championships, the school should consider seriously the claims of the club, and at all costs, the consequent good of the swimmer in question. This priority applies to the swimmer and his school and not to a Schools Swimming Association.

116. Championships.

116.1 The word 'Championship' shall be used only in connection with the championships of the A.S.A., a District Association, a County Association, or one of the bodies directly affiliated to the A.S.A. It may also be used in connection with the name of a locality, to which area entries to the championship shall be confined.

116.2 A club may promote a championship confined to its own members, and it may promote an open championship, in which case the title shall be qualified by the addition of a local name. The

District shall decide the title and rules governing a local championship.

117. Mixed Competitions. With

the following exceptions, a contest between the sexes shall not take place in public:

117.1 a team race or team diving contest in which each team consists of the same number of members each sex as each other team.

117.2 a school contest confined to school children under the age of sixteen years.

118. Masters Competitions.

118.1 Competitions held under A.S.A. Laws where competitors are required to be 25 years and over on the day of the competition shall be designated as Masters Competitions. Persons who are not eligible to compete under Law 101 who are members of affiliated clubs may compete if the promoter's rules so provide. They shall be subject to the same rules and conditions as the eligible competitors.

118.2 Where Masters competitions are held concurrently with other Championships and competitions, swimmers under the age of 25 years must not compete with or be seeded with Masters competitors.

119. Underwater Competitions/ Exhibitions.

119.1 No underwater competition or exhibition shall take place at any event promoted under A.S.A.Laws unless such is undertaken by an approved Sub-Aqua organisation which will be responsible for carrying out the necessary safeguards.

119.2 Where there are underwater movements in a swimming, diving water polo or synchronised swimming event these do not constitute an underwater competition but the competitors shall at all times be within the view of the officials.

120. Competitions by Children.

A child under the age of nine as on 31st December in the year of competition shall not take part in any open event held under A.S.A. Laws (see also Law 313).

121. Costumes.

121.1 The costumes of all competitors shall be in good moral taste and suitable for the individual sports discipline.

121.2 All costumes shall be non-transparent.

121.3 The referee of a competition has the authority to exclude any competitor whose costume does not comply with this rule.

LAWS OF THE SPORT

122. Smoking ban. At all events promoted by the A.S.A. smoking shall nt be permitted in any area designated for competitors, either prior to or during competitions.

123. Banned drugs

123.1 A competitor in an event under A.S.A Laws shall not use any drug or other substance which is on the F.I.N.A. List of Banned Substances in force at the time of the competition.

123.2 It shall be an offence for any person other than a medical practitioner treating him to aid, abet or incite a competitor to use a banned substance. Offenders shall be reported to the Chairman of the NJT.

123.3 A copy of the current F.I.N.A. List of Banned Substances shall be available to each competitor in any competition where drug testing is to be carried out.

124. Drug Testing

124.1 A swimmer in an open competition or a training session where random drug testing is to be carried out shall submit to a test for banned substances if selected to do so by the medical officer appointed to control the drug testing.

For a swimmer under 16 who is not registered, a form of consent to

a test shall be given by his parent or guardian in the following terms:

'I agree to my son/daughter/ward; if selected, being submitted to the medical procedure approved by the Amateur Swimming Association and to his submitting a sample of urine for analysis by the accredited laboratory.
Date.................Signed...............Parent/ Guardian'

124.2 The tests shall be carried out in accordance with regulations approved and published by the A.S.A. Committee.

124.3 If a swimmer who has been selected for a drug test refuses to submit to it, he shall be regarded as having been tested and a positive result obtained without extenuating circumstances.

124.4 A swimmer who is receiving medical treatment or who is taking drugs prescribed by the doctor must report the fact to the medical officer before the competition starts. If this is not done, a claim that a positive test result arose from prescribed medication will not be considered.

124.5 If a test reveals the presence of a body fluid of a banned drug, or one of its major metabolites, the fact will be reported by the medical officer controlling the test to the Chairman of the NJT, the promoter of the competition or training session and the Secretary of the

Medical Advisory Committee as prima facie evidence of the offence.

124.6 The Medical Officer controlling the test will arrange a meeting in accordance with Law 42.2 and advise the Chairman of the NJT of its opinion as to the existence of extenuating circumstances or otherwise.

124.7 The promoter will advise the swimmer of the result of the test but will take no further action until advised by the Chairman of the NJT.

125. Referees shall be appointed for all competitions. Their duties shall be those specified in the Rules and Conditions relating to the disciplines concerned together with the following:-

125.1 Have full control and authority over all officials: he shall approve their assignments and shall instruct them regarding any special features or regulations relating to the competition. He shall enforce all A.S.A Laws and the promoter's conditions governing the competition and shall decide any question relating to the actual conduct of the meeting, event or competition which is not covered by them,

125.2 have authority to intervene in the competition at any stage to ensure that A.S.A. Laws and the promoter's conditions governing the competition are compiled with,

125.3 ensure, before the commencement of the competition, that all the officials necessary for its conduct are present. He may appoint substitutes for officials who are absent, incapable of acting or found to be inefficient, and may appoint additional officials if he considers it necessary,

125.4 receive any protest which may be made. If a Jury of Appeal has been appointed, he shall report the protest to the Chairman of the Jury. If no Jury of Appeal has been appointed he shall ascertain the relevant facts and endeavour to resolve the matter.

If this is not practicable he shall report the facts and his action to the promoter. The competition shall be swum under protest and each of the competitors in the event informed of this. All medals or prizes shall be withheld until the protest and any appeal arising has been heard.

126. Jury of Appeal.

126.1 The promoter of an open competition may, if he so desires, appoint a Jury of Appeal to deal with any protests which may be made. Such a jury shall comprise three persons who are on or who have served on a District List who shall not undertake any other duties at the meeting.

126.2 The hearing shall take place as soon as it is practicable after the protest has been received and the provisions of Law 208.5 and 208.6 shall not apply.

127. Prizes All prizes for an open competition shall be purchased before the competition is held, and shall be of full advertised value. A competitor, being of opinion that his prize is not of the full advertised value, may protest to the referee of the competition, as provided in Law 208.

128. Trophies. Trophies can be either perpetual or challenge trophies. The conditions governing a competition for which a trophy is awarded shall state whether it is a challenge or a perpetual trophy:

128.1 A perpetual trophy may be held by the winner for a specified period only. It remains in the ownership of the body awarding it and cannot be won outright.

128.2 A challenge trophy is one presented for periodical competition until it has been won a stipulated number of times by the same competitor whose property it then becomes. Until won outright it may be held for a specified period only and it . remains in the ownership of the body awarding it.

128.3 The holder of a challenge trophy shall be given at least 21 days' notice of the closing date for entry to the next competition for it.

128.4 The rules of the competition for a challenge trophy shall not be changed without the consent of the holder if at that time he remains eligible to compete for it. If he is no longer eligible or if he cannot reasonably be traced, such consent must be obtained from a majority of past holders who remain eligible to compete and who can reasonably be traced.

128.5 The owner of the trophy shall be responsible for its insurance against loss while in the keeping for the holder.

129. Television. No swimming event, involving payment of a fee is to be televised without the prior sanction of the Amateur Swimming Association.

130. Testimonial or Benefit Galas

130.1 An affiliated club wishing to hold a gala, contest or exhibition in aid of a person or a charity cause other than its own fund, shall inform the District Hon. Secretary at least fourteen days before the meeting is to be held.

130.2 A copy of the financial statement, duly audited shall be sent to the District Hon. Secretary within one month of the meeting. An affiliated club which fails to comply with this Law shall become immediately suspended until such time as the matter has been dealt with by the District.

INTERNATIONAL EVENTS AND QUALIFICATION

131. International Competitions

are those in which the teams taking part have been selected by the governing bodies of the sport in the countries which they represent.

They shall be held under the Laws of the Federation Internationale de Natation Amateur, (F.I.N.A.).

132. English Qualification

132.1 A team may only be designated as an English team and represent England if it has been selected and managed by the A.S.A.

131.2 Anyone wishing to swim for England shall be an individual of British nationality and born in England, or born of English parents, or a naturalised British citizen who shall have lived continuously in England for at least one year.

132.3 If a competitor has represented England it is to be considered that he has chosen an English qualification and he will be under the control of the A.S.A. and cannot represent another country until he officially changes his national qualification.

132.4 A competitor wishing to change his national qualification from one national governing body to the A.S.A. shall have lived continuously in England and been under the jurisdiction of the A.S.A. for at least one year and may thereafter apply to the Secreatary of the A.S.A. for a change of national qualification.

132.5 A member of an affiliated club may join a club affiliated to another F.I.N.A. member. When competing in the competitions of the foreign club he shall be under the jurisdiction of that club and its national association.

132.6 A competitor who has two natinalities according to the laws of the representative nations shall, for the purpose of international competition, choose one national qualification and be under the control of the governing body of the chosen country.

132.7 A body affiliated to the A.S.A. under Law 5 shall not also be affiliated to any other member of the F.I.N.A.

133. Foreign Tours

133.1 Only members of the A.S.A., as defined in Law 3, who are registered with the A.S.A. may compete in any competition in a country outside Great Britain which is a member of F.I.N.A. The laws of the F.I.N.A. Member under which the competition is held shall apply.

133.2 Notice of all tours abroad shall be given to the Secretary of the A.S.A. at least 1 month before the tour starts giving full details of the itinerary and the names and

LAWS OF THE SPORT

registration numbers of those likely to take part.

Additional swimmers may also be included in the tour providing their names and registration numbers are given to the Secretary of the A.S.A. prior to departure.

133.3 All such teams or individual swimmers or officials shall remain within the jurisdiction of the A.S.A. during the period of time from their departure from until their return to England. Any team, individual swimmer, or official alleged to have been guilty of misbehaviour or unfair practice during such a period, shall, within 30 days of such return, be reported to the Secretary of the A.S.A., who shall bring the report to the notice of the A.S.A. Committee. In such cases that Committee shall have all the powers vested in a District Judicial Tribunal.

133.4 The Secretary of the A.S.A. having established that the arrangements are in order shall issue a permit.

134. Visits and Tours of Swimmers from outside Great Britain

134.1 Clubs or individuals arranging for the visits of swimmers from outside Great Britain shall submit particulars of the proposed arrangements to the Secretary of the A.S.A. before such arrangements are definitely concluded, and he in

turn shall furnish such information to the District Association of the Club or clubs concerned. The information required is:

134.1.1 the name of the club promoting and responsible for the visit,

134.1.2 an assurance that the visit has been approved by the National Association to which the visiting club is affiliated,

134.1.3 the financial arrangements,

134.1.4 a certificate from the National Association that all competing members of a visiting team are eligible

134.1.5 any other information requested by the Secretary of the A.S.A.

134.2 In the case of a water-polo match, the A.S.A. Water Polo Committee shall appoint the referee at the expense of the promoter unless a referee from a country not concerned is agreed upon by the competing clubs.

135. Home International Representation. No swimmer shall ever represent more than one of the Home Counties except:

135.1 In the case of the Commonwealth Games where if a swimmer has dual qualification for the Commonwealth Games, or the

qualification for his first international country has lapsed, he may be chosen for another country in these Games with the permission of the first 'international' country.

135.2 If a swimmer has been resident in another Home Country for a minimum period of twelve months he may represent that country provided his first international country agrees.

115

LAWS OF THE SPORT

SUSPENSION

232. A person under suspension shall not participate in any swimming activity organised by an affiliated club or controlled by A.S.A. Laws. He shall not act as a representative of a club or other affiliated body nor shall he be a member of any committee, sub-committee or council concerned with the direction or government of amateur swimming. He shall not act as an official at any competition, exhibition, meeting or any other activities within the sport.

233. A swimmer, club or official taking part in a competition held by an affiliated club or body, except as permitted in Laws 106 and 112, shall be suspended for such a period as the District Judicial Tribunal shall direct.

234. An eligible competitor taking part in a competition, exhibition or demonstration with one whom he knows to be under suspension shall himself be suspended for such a period as the District Judicial Tribunal shall direct.

235. Suspensions by a District Judicial Tribunal or the National Judicial Tribunal shall be binding on all clubs, County Associations, District Associations and bodies affiliated directly to the A.S.A. and shall be reported to F.I.N.A. for recognition worldwide.

236. The registration card of a suspended registered person shall be withdrawn by the DJT and forwarded to the Registrar. He may at the end of his suspension, apply to the Registrar for his card to be returned, unless it has expired, when he may make a fresh application for registration.

237. Club Suspensions. For a breach of its own rules, an affiliated club may suspend a member from activities wholly within its own jurisdiction provided that, before doing so, it informs the member of the alleged offence and gives him a reasonable opportunity to defend himself against the charge. If the alleged offence is also an offence against A.S.A. Law, the club shall not deal with it but shall report the facts to the Chairman of the DJT in accordance with Law 210.

LAWS OF RACING

301. Officials

301.1 A decision of the Referee on a question of fact shall be final, except in regard to placings where an agreed decision on placings by the placing judges shall be final.

301.2 Where the placing judges disagree, the decision of the Referee on the placings where they differ shall be final.

301.3 Where approved automatic judging and timing equipment, including any secondary system associated with it, is in use, the decision of the Referee on the correctness of its operation shall be final.

301.4 The Referee's application of the A.S.A. Laws and the promoter's conditions must be accepted at the time, but may be the subject of a protest.

301.5 Judges shall not act as timekeepers in the same event.

301.6 A professional may act as an official in any swimming contest under the A.S.A. Laws, subject to those conditions governing the appointment of amateur officials.

301.7 For all open competitions there shall be:

301.7.1 A Referee.

LAWS OF THE SPORT

301.7.2 A Starter.

301.7.3 A Check Starter for handicap races.

301.7.4 Not less than two Placings Judges and such additional judges as may be necessary to bring to the notice of the referee any instance in which a swimmer fails to comply with A.S.A. Laws or the promoter's conditions during a race.

301.7.5 Not less than two Turning Judges for each turning or take-over line other than the finishing line.

301.7.6 A Chief Timekeeper and at least one Timekeeper for each lane, except in a competition where times are not required for determining race results.

301.7.7 Competitors' Stewards.

301.7.8 A Recorder.

302. Duties and Powers of Officials

302.1 THE REFEREE shall:

302.1.1 give a decision in accordance with Law 303.2.5 when the placings of the judges are inconsistent with the timings by the timekeepers,

302.1.2 give a decision where the appropriate officials fail to agree. In cases where the placings judges disagree, he shall give a

decision on the placings that differ,

302.1.3 before each event, satisfy himself that all the competitors and officials are in their places and aware that the event is about to start and signal to the starter when he is so satisfied,

302.1.4 disqualify any competitor for any violation of the rules that he personally observes or which is reported to him by other authorised officials and inform the placing judges, after consultation with the officials concerned.

302.2 THE STARTER shall:

302.2.1 in a minor competition, where authorised by the referee, satisfy himself that the competitors are on their correct stations and are aware of what they have to do,

302.2.2 have control of the competitors from the time they are handed over to him by the referee until a valid start has been made,

302.2.3 with the concurrence of the referee, disqualify competitors for delaying the start, for disobeying an order or for any other misconduct taking place at the start,

302.2.4 have power to decide whether the start is valid, subject only to the decision of the Referee

302.2.5 have the power to recall the competitors at any time after the signal to start has been given in accordance with Law 304.2.1.

302.3 THE CHECK STARTER shall:

in a handicap event, disqualify any competitor who starts before his number is called unless he returns to his starting place on the side of the bath or in the water under his original station and starts afresh.

He shall report such disqualification to the Referee.

302.4 THE CHIEF TIMEKEEPER shall:

302.4.1 before the commencement of the competition, arrange for a check on the accuracy of the watches to be used,

302.4.2 assign each timekeeper to the lane for which he will be responsible,

302.4.3 if necessary, direct a reserve timekeeper to time the lane of the timekeeper whose watch fails to start, stops prematurely or who for any other reason is unable to record the time. Should there be no reserve timekeeper available, he should time the lane himself.

302.4.4 collect from each timekeeper the time recorded, record the official time for each lane and report it to the referee,

117

LAWS OF THE SPORT

302.4.5 inspect the watches, if necessary, and after each event give a signal when the watches are to be reset.

302.5 A TIMEKEEPER shall:

302.5.1 take the time of the competitor assigned to him by starting his watch when the starting signal is given and stopping it when the competitor has completed the course,

302.5.2 after each race, and before consulting with any other timekeepers on his lane, record the time on his report card,

302.5.3 present his watch for inspection if requested. He shall not reset his watch until he receives the signal from the Chief Timekeeper,

302.5.4 wherever possible, for events of 400m or longer except for relays and medley events, record the number of laps completed by his competitor and keep him informed of the remaining laps to be completed by displaying for observation of the competitor at the finishing end of the pool, lap cards bearing numbers.

302.5.5 give a warning signal when his competitor has two lengths plus 5m to swim to the finish in events of 400m or longer except for relays or medley events. The warning signal may be a pistol shot, whistle or bell.

302.6 THE PLACING JUDGES shall:

302.6.1 take up positions where, in all events and at all times, they have a clear view of the whole of the course and be in line with the finish when it is taking place,

302.6.2 with the concurrence of the Referee, disqualify for fouling,

302.6.3 act as turning judges at the finishing line,

302.6.4 after each event, individually record and then decide the order of finishing and report it to the Referee.

302.7 THE TURNING JUDGES shall:

report to the referee any competitor who, between the commencement of the last armstroke before touching for the turn or take over and the end of the first armstroke after the turn, fails to comply with the relevant A.S.A Laws. In Breaststroke events the Turning Judges shall be responsible for observing the competitor until his head has broken the surface of the water after the turn.

302.8 THE STROKE JUDGES shall:

report to the referee any competitor who fails to comply with A.S.A. Law regarding the stroke conditions of the competition.

302.9 THE COMPETITORS' STEWARDS shall:

302.9.1 wear a distinguishing badge,

302.9.2 be responsible for behaviour in the dressing rooms and report misbehaviour to the referee,

302.9.3 be responsible, where necessary, for arranging the competitors into heats,

302.9.4 be responsible for ensuring that the competitors are on the correct stations prior to each event, (but see 302.2.1),

302.9.5 carry out any duties delegated by the Referee in respect of any entry card system in operation for that competition.

302.10 THE RECORDER shall:

302.10.1 record the places and times on a results sheet when the race results are handed to him,

302.10.2 extract the names of the swimmers for any swim-off or the final and arrange them in accordance with A.S.A Law,

302.10.3 arrange for the early announcement of the names of swimmers for any swim-off or the final so that they may be warned and, when this has been done, pass the list of names so announced to the other officials concerned.

303. Decision of the Times and Placings

303.1 Using Automatic Judging and Timing Equipment

303.1.1 Automatic judging and timing equipment is equipment which is started by the starting signal and is stopped by the competitor at the end of the course.

303.1.2 Where approved automatic judging and timing equipment has been provided, it shall be used to determine the winner and placings and the times for each lane. The results and times so determined shall have precedence over the decisions of human judges and timekeepers provided the Referee is satisfied that it operated correctly. Where the approved system incorporates a secondary recording system, which supports the primary system, and is started by the same starting equipment as the primary system but terminated by appointed timekeepers, the times recorded by the secondary system shall be deemed official times in the event of failure of the approved primary equipment.

303.1.3 Where there is any failure in the whole, or in part, of the approved equipment the following procedure shall be adopted:

303.1.3.1 Record all available automatic times and places.

303.1.3.2 Record all human times and places.

The official times for all competitors having automatically recorded times shall be those times. The official times for all competitors not having automatically recorded times shall be manually recorded times.

303.1.4 To determine the official place and time of a competitor in a race, the following procedure shall apply:

303.1.4.1 A competitor having an automatically recorded place must retain that place in relation to other competitors having automatically recorded places.

303.1.4.2 A competitor not having an automatically recorded place but having an automatically recorded time shall be given a place in the order of finishing by comparing that time with the automatically recorded times of other competitors.

303.1.4.3 No automatically recorded order of finishing may be altered, except that all competitors having the same automatically recorded time shall be tied in the order of finishing.

303.1.4.4 A competitor having

neither an automatically recorded place nor an automatically recorded time shall be given a place in the order of finishing in accordance with the human placings. He shall be given the manually recorded time, adjusted as necessary in accordance with Law 303.2.5, with a zero added in the second decimal place if necessary.

303.1.4.5 A competitor having an automatically recorded place but not having an automatically recorded time shall retain that place in the order of finishing. His time shall be determined by reference to his manually recorded time.

303.1.5 When approved automatic timing to 1/1000th of a second is used, the third decimal place shall not be recorded or used; all competitors making the same time by the operation of this law shall be considered tied.

303.1.5.1 When approved automatic timing to 1/100th of a second is used, the timings shall be as recorded.

303.2 Using Human Judges and Timekeepers

303.2.1 Crystal controlled handheld electronic timers are recognised for record purposes; provided that the crystal has an

LAWS OF THE SPORT

accuracy of thirty parts in a million or better. Timers with L.E.D. displays must be fitted with a means of checking the battery. Timers with L.C.D type must have the battery renewed in a period of not exceeding twelve months irrespective of the battery used. Such electronic timers are not to be regarded as approved electronic timing apparatus, as referred to previously. They shall be read to 1/100th of a second when all the watches concerned are designated electronic timers. When they are used in conjunction with watches they shall be read to 1/10th of a second, and where there is a second decimal point other than '0' the time shall be raised to the next highest 10th.

303.2.2 Where three timekeepers are used for a lane, if the times recorded by two timekeepers agree, that shall be the accepted time, but in cases where the times recorded by all three timekeepers disagree, that recorded by the middle watch shall be accepted.

303.2.3 Where two timekeepers are used for a lane, if the times recorded do not agree, then the slower of the times recorded shall be the accepted time.

303.2.4 Where one timekeeper only is used for a lane, then his recorded time shall be the

accepted time.

303.2.5 If the times registered by the timekeepers do not agree with the decision of the placing judges, the times for the competitors concerned shall be added together and divided by the number of such competitors who shall be credited with that time, raised, if necessary to the nearest tenth or hundredth (as appropriate under paragraph 303.2.1) of a second slower. It is not permissible to announce times which do not support the classifications made by the placing judges.

303.3 Disqualification

303.3.1 Should a competitor be disqualified during an event, such disqualifications shall be recorded in the official results but no time or place shall be recorded.

303.3.2 A disabled swimmer shall not be disqualified in a competition, in a case where his disability prevents him from complying with the rules of a particular stroke.

304. Starting

304.1 Starts

304.1.1 Where the promoters decide and so publish in the rules of the competition and publicly announce at the event, the procedure detailed in Law 304.2.2 and 304.2.3 may be suspended in that a swimmer shall be

disqualified for any false start as defined in Law 304.2.1.

304.1.2 The starter shall, when starting an event, take up a position on the side of the pool where the competitors can hear the starting signal and the timekeepers can see or hear it.

304.1.3 The referee shall signal that the event is about to start by a series of short sharp blasts on his whistle. When he is satisfied that the competitors and the appropriate officials are ready, he shall give a single, long blast whereupon the competitors starting from the side of the pool shall take up their positions on the back of the starting block or a short pace back from the starting line and competitors starting in the water shall immediately enter the water and take up their positions for the start. The referee shall then signal to the starter, by means of a raised hand, that he may proceed to start the race. In a minor competition where the Referee deems it expedient he may delegate his functions in relation to the start to the Starter.

304.1.4 on the preparatory command from the starter 'Take your marks', the competitors shall immediately take up a starting position either on the front of the starting blocks or line, or as required to conform to the relevant parts of A.S.A laws 307, 308, 309, and 310 and shall remain stationary until the starter gives the starting signal.

304.1.5 In a scratch race, the starting signal may be by shot, whistle, the word 'Go' or klaxon. In handicap races the starting signal shall be given by the word 'Go' followed by the counting of the seconds until all the competitors in the race have started.

304.1.6 For deaf swimmers, the starter should make adequate provision after consultation with the competitors or their representatives.

304.2 False Starts in Scratch Races

304.2.1 If after the command 'take your marks', a swimmer leaves his starting place before or is moving when, the starting signal is given it shall be a false start.

304.2.2 In the event of a first or second start:

304.2.2.1 the starter shall call back the swimmers by repeating the starting signal, whereupon the false start rope shall be dropped.

304.2.2.2 if the Referee decides that a start is false,

although the Starter has decided that it was valid, he shall blow his whistle, whereupon the starter shall repeat the starting signal.

304.2.2.3 After two false starts in a race the Starter shall warn the swimmers that at the third attempt the race will proceed, irrespective of further infringement, and any swimmer who is not stationary in his starting position when the starting signal is given will be disqualified by the starter, whether or not he was a previous offender.

304.3 Wherever Practical

304.3.1 A rope shall be provided to stop the swimmers in the event of a false start.

304.3.2 It shall be suspended across the pool from fixed stands 15m in front of the starting end, attached to the stands by a quick release mechanism.

304.3.3 If the rope is not operated automatically by the repetition of the starting signal it shall be released by a designated official in response to that signal.

305. Heats and Finals

305.1 When the number of competitors exceeds the number of lanes available, heats, any necessary swim off to resolve ties, and a final, shall be swum or alternatively results may be decided on heat time classification, without finals, if the conditions of the competition are so agreed and published. To be eligible for the final of an event, a competitor must have competed in the heats, if any.

305.2 Except with the consent of all competitors affected, a heat or final shall not be started before the advertised time, if any, of starting, or the stipulated interval, if any, between rounds has elapsed.

305.3 When all events at a gala start at the same end of the pool, stations shall count from the right facing the course from the starting end. When the events at the gala do not all start from the same end of the pool but all events finish at the same end of the pool, stations shall count from the right facing the course from the finishing end.

305.4 Heats

305.4.1 *Scratch races.* The promoter, at his option, shall arrange the programme order of the competitors by draw or by seeding on times given on the entry forms.

305.4.2 *Handicap races.* The promoter shall arrange the competitors in handicap order, or in heats in handicap order, with the limit competitor (being the one who has the longest start) on the right facing the course.

305.4.3 Where heats are necessary the finalists shall be the competitors accomplishing the fastest times in the heats, subject where necessary to the concurrence of the judges as to placing in the heats. Where the number of finalists exceeds the number of available lanes by reason of a dead heat or equal time, unless the promoters conditions allow for a lesser number of finalists than there are lanes in the pool, all the competitors concerned in a dead heat or equal time shall swim off for the remaining lane(s).

305.4.4 In handicap races the qualifying time shall be the gross time of the competitor concerned.

305.5 Finals

305.5.1 *Scratch races.* The stations of the competitors shall be decided on the spearhead system which provides that the competitor who qualified with the fastest time in the heats is stationed in the centre lane and the other competitors in the remaining lanes on the left and right alternatively according to their respective times.

305.5.2 *Handicap races.* The competitors shall be placed in handicap order.

305.5.3 In the event of a dead heat in the final, the competitors may, with the consent of the referee, divide the prize or prizes, or compete again at such time and place as he may direct.

305.6 Team Races

305.6.1 The rules relating to heats and finals shall apply to team events, except that swimmers may be freely interchanged for each round.

305.6.2 The team of a competitor whose feet, or hands in the case of a swimmer starting in the water, have lost touch with his starting place before his preceding partner touches the end shall be disqualified, unless the competitor in default returns to his starting place at the wall. It shall not be necessary to remount the starting platform. Running takeovers are not permitted.

305.6.3 A swimmer in a team race shall not be permitted to swim more than one leg.

306. The Race

306.1 Swimming Over. When only one competitor reports for an event he shall, to qualify as the winner, complete the whole distance and comply with the laws governing style, turning and finishing.

306.2 Standing or Walking. A competitor may not walk during a race.

He may - in a Freestyle race only - stand for the purpose of resting.

306.3 Fouling. A foul is any action by a swimmer as a result of which another swimmer in the same event suffers an unfair disadvantage. Should a foul endanger the chance of success of a competitor, the referee shall have power to allow him to compete in the final. Should a foul occur in a final, the referee may order it to be re-swum. Should the foul be intentional the referee shall report the matter to the Chairman of the District Judicial Tribunal (Law 204).

306.4 In all events when turning, a swimmer is not permitted to take a stride or step from the bottom of the pool nor may he leave the water.

306.5 Where there are lane ropes, a swimmer must finish in the lane in which he started. A breaststroke swimmer shall not be disqualified if he submerges for not more than one stroke for the purpose of returning to his lane.

306.6 Goggles may be worn.

306.7 After completing the race a swimmer must remain in the water in his own lane until released by the referee or other official authorised by him.

306.8 Illegal Pool Entry
306.8.1 A non-competitor who,

in the opinion of the Referee or a judge, deliberately enters the water while a race is in progress, except to go to the assistance of a swimmer in distress, shall be reported by the Referee to the Chairman of the DJT. Anyone whose deliberate action causes someone to enter the water involuntarily during a race shall be similarly reported.

306.8.2 A relay team shall be disqualified from a race if a member of the team enters the water while the race is in progress unless he does so for the purpose of starting his leg.

307 Freestyle. A competitor may start with a plunge or jump, or in the water holding the rail or side of the pool or other starting place. A competitor may swim any style or styles and rules relating specifically to Breaststroke, Butterfly, and Backstroke swimming shall not apply. In Freestyle turning and finishing the swimmer may touch the wall with any part of his body.

308. Breaststroke

308.1 A competitor may start with a plunge or jump, or in the water, facing the course, and holding the rail or side of the pool or other starting place, with both hands.

308.2 From the beginning of the first arm stroke after the start and after each turn the body shall be kept on the breast and the

shoulders shall be in line with (parallel to) the water surface.

308.3 All movements of the hands and feet shall be simultaneous and in the same horizontal plane without alternating movement except at each turn and upon the finish of the race when the touch may be made with the hands at different levels.

308.4 hands shall be pushed forward together from the breast, and shall be brought back on or under the surface of the water. Except at the start and at the turns, the hands shall not be brought back beyond the hip line.

308.5 In the leg kick the feet shall be turned outward in the backward movement. Up or down movements of the legs or feet in the vertical plane in the form of a 'dolphin' kick are not permitted.

308.6 At each turn and upon the finish of the race, the touch shall be made with both hands simultaneously, not necessarily at the same level, either at, above or below the water level. The shoulders shall remain in the horizontal plane.

308.7 During each complete cycle of one arm stroke and one leg kick, some part of the head of the swimmer shall break the surface of the water, except that after the start and after each turn the swimmer may take one arm stroke completely back to the legs and

one leg kick while wholly submerged before returning to the surface.

FINA Interpretation of the Breaststroke Law

After the start and after each turn, the swimmer is permitted, as previously, to take one arm stroke completely back to the legs and return the arms to the original forward position, followed by one leg kick, while wholly submerged. The head must break the surface of the water during the first part of the second arm stroke, that is, before the hands begin to turn inward at the widest part of the second arm stroke.

During each cycle after the first, part of the swimmer's head must actually come out of the water. It is no longer sufficient for the head to remain above the level of the calm water surface, with the possibility of a wave covering the top of the head. It is important that part of the head actually be exposed directly to the air.

FINA Rule SW 7.3 now explicitly states that the hands may not come down beyond the hipline after the first armstroke at the completion of the start and each turn. This does not represent a drastic departure from the previous rule, but is merely intended to ensure that throughout the race the swimmer does not glide underwater with the arms flat or nearly flat against the side of the body, as is normal after the start and turns. The swimmer should get the benefit of any doubt relating to the position of the hipline.

LAWS OF THE SPORT

Although the rule has not changed, there has been inconsistent interpretation of SW 7.3 regarding the recovery portion of the armstroke. The hands must be pushed forward together from the breast on, under, or over the water. A butterfly-style recovery is not permissible.

At each turn and at the finish, the swimmer no longer must touch with his hands at the same level. However, the rule that the shoulders must remain in the horizontal plane has not changed. The head may now be submerged immediately prior to the turn or finish, so long as the head broke the surface of the water at some point during the cycle preceding the turn or finish.

309. Butterfly

309.1 A competitor may start with a plunge or jump, or in the water, facing the course, and holding the rail, or side of the pool or other starting place, with both hands.

309.2 All movements of the hands shall be simultaneous. The arms should be brought forward over the water and brought back on or under the surface.

309.3 The body shall be kept on the breast with the shoulders horizontal from the beginning of the first arm stroke after the start and after the turn.

309.4 All movements of the feet shall be executed in a

simultaneous manner. Simultaneous up and down movements of the legs and feet in the vertical plane are permitted. The legs or feet need not be at the same level but no alternating movement is permitted.

309.5 At each turn and upon the finish of the race, the touch shall be made with both hands, simultaneously, either at, above or below the water level. The shoulders shall remain in the horizontal plane.

309.6 At the start and at turns, a swimmer is permitted one or more leg kicks and one arm pull under the water, which shall bring him to the surface.

310. Backstroke

310.1 Competitors shall line up in the water facing the starting end with hands on the end, rail, or starting grips. The feet, including the toes, shall be under the surface of the water. Standing in or on the gutter or bending the toes over the lip of the gutter is prohibited.

310.2 At the starting signal they shall push off and swim on their backs throughout the race, except during turns. The hands shall not be released before the starting signal has been given. While required to be on the back, the shoulders of the competitors shall not roll more than 90° from the horizontal.

310.3 When touching at the turn and at the finish, the touch shall be made by the head, shoulder, foremost hand or arm. The turn shall begin when the competitor correctly touches the end of the course at the push off.

310.4 Wherever possible backstroke turn indicators shall be provided by means of flagged ropes suspended across the pool 1.8m above the water surface from fixed supports or stands set 5m from each end wall of the pool.

310.5 Clarification of Turn: it is permissible to turn over beyond the vertical after the foremost part of the body has touched, for the purpose of executing the turn, but the swimmer shall have returned past the vertical to a position on his back before the feet have left the wall.

311. Medley Events shall consist of equal legs on four strokes in the following order:-
Individual Medley - Butterfly, Backstroke, Breaststroke, Freestyle.
Medley Relay - Backstroke, Breaststroke, Butterfly, Freestyle.

In Medley events, Freestyle shall be any stroke other than Butterfly, Backstroke, or Breaststroke.

312. Handicap Races.

312.1 An official handicapper may be appointed by each District. A District may delegate the appointment to a County Association.

312.2 An official handicapper may receive a fee in accordance with the scale authorised by the District.

312.3 Every open handicap shall be made by an official handicapper whose name and address, together with all particulars of the handicap shall be published in the programme of the event.

312.4 Only the official handicapper shall have power to alter a handicap he has made.

312.5 In all open handicaps, the starts shall be allotted from basal times at various distances, to be fixed by the A.S.A. Committee. **Note**: The basal times for 1989 shall be:

50 yards	Men	21	Women	24
50 metres	"	24	"	27
55 yards	"	24	"	27
66 2/3 yards	"	30	"	34
73 2/3 yards	"	33	"	38
100 yards	"	47	"	54
100 metres	"	53	"	59
100 yards	"	54	"	59

313. Racing by Children.

The minimum age at which a swimmer may take part in a swimming race under A.S.A. Laws shall be:

313.1 Events restricted to members of one club.
- No minimum age.

313.2.1 Open relay races other than in District and National Competitions.
- 9 years

313.2.2 inter-club events limited to not more than eight clubs which do not form part of a series of events as in a league.
- 9 years

313.3.1 Open individual events, other than in District, and National Competitions,
- 10 years

313.3.2 relay events in District Competitions.
- 10 years

313.4.1 individual events in District Competitions
- 11 years

313.4.2 relay events in National Competitions.
- 11 years

313.5 Individual events in National Competitions.
- 12 years

For all categories, the age shall be the age attained in the year of competition.

314. British and English Records

The following distances and strokes shall be recognised for British and English records:

Freestyle: 50, 100, 200, 400, 800 and 1500 metres

Backstroke: 50, 100 and 200 metres
Breaststroke: 50, 100 and 200 metres
Individual medley: 200 and 400 metres
Freestyle relay team: 4 x 100 and 4 x 200 metres
Medley relay team: 4 x 100 metres

All records shall be recognised for men and for women, for Long and Short course, and for open and junior age classification.
The conditions following shall apply:-

314.1 The Swimmers

314.1.1 For individual events swimmers must be British or English as appropriate in accordance with Law 132.

314.1.2 For team events:

314.1.2.1 For English records, the team members must all be English in accordance with Law 132 and the team must represent Great Britain, the A.S.A., one of its Districts, or a club affiliated thereto.

314.1.2.2 For British records, the team members must all be Briitish in accordance with Law 132 and the team must represent the A.S.A. or one of its Districts, the Scottish A.S.A., the Welsh A.S.A. (or any combinations thereof) or a club affiliated to one of those Associations.

314.1.3 Swimmers shall be eligible competitors.

LAWS OF THE SPORT

314.1.4 For junior records, swimmers shall be under sixteen years of age at all times of the swims. For open records there are no age limits.

314.1.5 Swimmers shall comply with the conditions of Law 121 as though members of both sexes were present.

314.2 The Pool

314.2.1 Short Course Records may be made only in pools of 25 metres or 27 1/2 yards in length. Long Course records may be made only in pools 50 metres or 55 yards in length.

314.2.2 The start and finish shall be at ends of the pool.

314.2.3 All records shall be made in still water. Any movement of water due to the\ normal operation of the filtration system may be diregarded.

314.2.4 The course shall be certified correct by an appropriate qualified person.

314.2.5 The height of the platform above the water surface shall not exceed 75cm.

314.3 The Event

314.3.1 A record may only be made in:

314.3.1.1 A scratch competition held in public under A.S.A. Laws

provided that the Referee, Starter, judges and timekeepers are on the panel of the District, or

314.3.1.2 an unplaced individual race against time held in public provided that the date and venue have been fixed and advertiscd as such before the day of the event and the Referee, Starter, judges and time-keepers are on the panel of a District, or

314.3.1.3 a scratch competition held under the auspices and in accordance with the record conditions of the Scottish or Welsh A.S.A., or of any country affiliated to F.I.N.A., provided that the rekevant conditions of this Law are complied with.

314.3.2 A swimmer in an individual event may apply for a record at an intermediate distance if he, his coach, or his manager requests the Referee that his performance be timed at that distance which must be from the start of the event. The swimmer must complete the scheduled distance of the event without disqualification.

314.3.3 The first swimmer in a relay event may apply for a record at an intermediate distance if he, his coach or his manager requests the Referee that his performance be timed at that distance. Such performance shall not be nullified by any disqualification of his team or team members occurring after his leg is completed.

314.4 Timing

314.4.1 The time shall be taken by automatic judging and timing equipment approved by the appropriate national governing body of swimming or, if this is not available by three timekeepers, using electronic hand timers reading to 1/100th of a second and complying with A.S.A. Law 303.2.

314.4.2 The procedures of Law 302.5 and Law 303.1 and 2 shall apply except for those concerned with two or one human timekeeper.

314.4.3 When human timekeepers are used, the Chief Timekeeper or Referee shall inspect the timers used and record the times. The accepted time shall be publicly announced.

314.5 Application, Ratification and Publication

314.5.1 All records must be applied for on the official form obtainable from the A.S.A. Application shall be made within fourteen days of this event.

314.5.2 For records set by a swimmer or relay team when competing as members of an A.S.A. or Great Britain team the application should be made by the Team Manager or by someone appointed by him for that purpose.

314.5.3 For records set at championships or competitions promoted by the A.S.A., the applications should be made by the Referee or by someone appointed for that purpose.

314.5.4 For records set overseas, the applications should be made by the Referee or by someone appointed for that purpose.

314.5.5 For records set in Great Britain, the application shall be sent to the Hon. Secretary of the District or of the Scottish or Welsh A.S.A. as appropriate to the venue of the event concerned and shall be forwarded by him to the Secretary of the A.S.A.

314.5.6 The Secretary of the A.S.A. shall arrange for ratification of English records by the A.S.A. Committee and for the approval of British records for ratification by the Committee of the A.S.F. of G.B. in accordance with their constitution. He shall publish details of new records at the first suitable opportunity.

314.5.7 A complete list of British and English records as at 31st December shall be printed inthe next following A.S.A. Handbook.

314.5.8 A certificate shall be awarded by the A.S.A. for each new record made.

314.6 The Secretary of the A.S.A. shall scrutinise all applications for English records and forward to the appropriate body any that appear to be European, Commonwealth or World Records, except where the

performances were achieved in the European Championships or other L.E.N. events, the Commonwealth Games or the World Championships respectively.

INTERPRETATION OF A.S.A. LAW

601. When interpretation of an A.S.A. law or the rules governing A.S.A. championships is required, or when any matter arises which is not covered by A.S.A. Law, it shall be referred to the A.S.A. Committee whose decision shall be immediately effective. If any question arises concerning a conflict between the A.S.A. Laws and/or the Rules of the District Association and/ or County Association it shall be referred to the A.S.A. Committee who shall refer it in accordance with Law 35 before making its decision, subject to the approval of the A.S.A. Council at its next meeting.

LAWS OF THE SPORT

THIS BOOK HAS SHOWN THE IMPORTANT AND WIDE-RANGING ROLE OF THE COACH. IT HAS ALSO INDICATED THE KNOWLEDGE REQUIRED TO BE AN EFFECTIVE AND SUCCESSFUL COACH. THE SCOPE OF THIS BOOK CANNOT COVER EVERY TOPIC IN DETAIL, SO IF YOU HAVE DEVELOPED AN INTEREST IN SOME ASPECT OF COACHING SUCH AS MENTAL PREPARATION, FITNESS TRAINING OR THE PREVENTION OF INJURY, THE **NATIONAL COACHING FOUNDATION**, ESTABLISHED TO PROVIDE A SERVICE FOR SPORTS COACHES, RUNS COURSES, PRODUCES STUDY PACKS, BOOKS, VIDEOS AND OTHER RESOURCES ON MANY PERFORMANCE RELATED AREAS PARTICULARLY DESIGNED FOR THE PRACTISING COACH.

CONTACT THE **NATIONAL COACHING FOUNDATION** AT: 4 COLLEGE CLOSE, BECKETT PARK, LEEDS LS6 3QH. TELEPHONE: LEEDS (0532) 744802

NOTE
READERS ARE REMINDED THAT LAWS OF SPORTS CHANGE FROM TIME TO TIME. IF COACHES ARE INVOLVED IN COMPETITION SWIMMING , THE CURRENT LAWS SHOULD ALWAYS BE CONSULTED FOR THE MOST UP-TO-DATE RULINGS. FAILURE TO DO THIS COULD SERIOUSLY DISADVANTAGE THEIR SWIMMERS IN COMPETITION.